DON'T SELL

—— THE ——

HORSE

INSPIRING STORIES OF
HEALTHCARE PROFESSIONALS

Collected by

Kessarin Panichpisal, M.D.

Copyright © 2022 Don't Sell The Horse
Published by Kessarin Panichpisal

Cover design by Ricacabrex (fiverr.com)

ISBN: 979-8-218-07331-2

Printed in the United States of America.

Library of Congress Cataloging-in-Publication Data
October 28, 2022

Names: Kessarin Panichpisal, Author
Title: Don't Sell The Horse
Description:
Identifiers: 979-8-218-07331-2 + Barcode
Subject: Inspirational / Healthcare

Illustrations by Katerina Dotneboya

DEDICATION

To my wonderful parents, teachers, and patients.

Contents

Foreword

An idea dies as a thought. I said this to myself many years ago as a means of finding motivation to keep setting goals and striving to achieve them. In a sense, this has become one of my personal mantras. While the concept of dying doesn't necessarily evoke pleasant imagery, the statement is meant to represent the important transition from being just an idea to having what that concept represents become a reality. When the product of our choices leads to actualization of an idea, it leads to innovation and invention, and a circumstance can evolve beyond where it starts. However, it isn't easy to pursue all of our dreams, partly out of sheer practicality, be it financial or grandiosity of scope, or strictly due to a fear of failure in attaining the goal. Ultimately, if we don't aspire to evoke more ideas, or find ways to pursue them, they will end only as unrealized possibilities.

This compilation of individuals' experiences came to fruition partly because of this concept, calling for action to make a thought a reality. Dr. Panichpisal and I have worked closely together for six years as partners helping to care for many critical patients, together experiencing many highs and lows. Incidentally, we had met two years earlier at a medical device user group meeting, when she was a new neurointerventional fellow. It was clear then that she was a compassionate, intelligent, and dedicated physician. As I've gotten to know her while working together, she is a model for providing empathic and inclusive care. The book's concept evolved from discussions we have had about the nature of our job and how it can impact our career satisfaction, along with reasons to continue to persevere.

My decision for entering healthcare evolved through many experiences. Growing up, school was challenging, though came somewhat easy for me. I can't say that I always wanted to become a doctor, or that there was a single event leading to my decision to become one. In a sense, I feel that the field chose me through a series of serendipitous events. Along the way, I had planned to be an engineer, a mathematician, a dentist and a biologist. I liked working with my hands and manual labor, though the pursuit of knowledge kept me going. By the time I was halfway through college, I maintained a substantial interest in research and basic science. It was around that time I took my first psychology course. Having already learned basic neurobiology by then, I became fascinated with how incredible the brain and nervous systems are. These events culminated in pursuit of medical school and hopes to become a neurosurgeon. Once in medical school I considered various other specialties, but discovered neurointerventional and saw the potential for the field. Since the time I decided on this specialty and started practicing in 2010, the field has gone through many changes and incredible advances. Outcomes and mortality have improved, though despite the advances, there remain both good and bad outcomes. While it is inherently easier to manage the good outcomes, bad outcomes can make us question whether pursuing a different path is best, but these situations can also be used to find ways to improve subsequent outcomes.

We all have had a "horse" that we have wanted to sell. Despite the most comprehensive plan, things don't always work out the way we want. This can lead to self-doubt over our original idea and reasons for having made a given choice. While the factors that motivate an individual's decisions can widely vary, they are often born out of thoughts we have for ourselves and from the emotions of those who we value in our lives. Greater societal factors can also play a role, which I believe is a result of humankind having an inherent ability for empathy. The challenges that we face in healthcare are not entirely specific to healthcare, but the constant experience of others' suffering can build, contributing to burn out and disengagement. Being mindful of our own limitations and the limitations of others, provides humility and an independent source of motivation.

When faced with adversity we need to remind ourselves that it may be easiest to "sell the horse." The reality though is that fighting in the face of adversity can make us stronger and lead to more resolve. It is common to face adversity. Setting realistic expectations for ourselves might help us cope with these challenges. It also seems important to recognize that despite best intentions and hope, things may not end up the way we want. In medicine, we may see this as progression of disease in the face of state of the art and even advanced experimental treatment. Considering life is full of challenges with successes and failures, our ideas and motivations will evolve with our personal experiences. We need to keep riding through our challenges and find a way to stay ahead of negativity, rather than selling the horse solely for going down an errant path.

~Thomas Wolfe MD

The faculty of language is one of the quintessential human assets. While all animal species possess some mode of intergroup communication, our spoken words have a great deal of making us who we are.

More than any other field of medicine perhaps, neurology delves into exactly that—those aspects which form the individual. The discovery of brain mechanisms of working has intrigued scientists and attracted great minds into the field for centuries.

The intricacies of neural networks and mechanisms continue to astound us. As a young medical student, ambitious and propelled by ambition and the love of a challenge, I immediately turned to neurology, for no other reason than I thought it would be the most difficult field to master. As I learned more, it became a true story of "love after marriage," where a growing reverence for the nervous system drew me towards learning how our mere thoughts and desires could translate into our bodies' motions, to attain a goal. Early in my residency I saw myself seeking a career in behavioral neurology, the subspecialty focusing on diseases such as Alzheimer's disease. In my naiveté I thought stroke to be too dry (like surgery, an equally misinformed assumption I held at that time), a disease process lacking subtlety or nuance the way other neurological diseases had. However, as often is the case, in the midst of the actual practice of neurology as a residency, I learned not just about field, but more about myself, and found that my inclination truly leaned towards stroke neurology. Here my patients taught me about myself.

Learning the details of the neurological examination— a standard curriculum among medical students— takes years to hone and perfect beyond postgraduate training and well into the attending level career. For years neurology had been dismissed by other specialists with the stereotype, "Diagnose and adios," a pejorative reference to the precise ability for a well-conducted clinical examination to pinpoint the location in the nervous system of the pathology, though without any real means of treatment. And stroke, one of the top causes of all cause morbidity and mortality worldwide and in the United States, led the charge in this, as a devastating disease, striking with life-altering suddenness and severity. The era of thrombolytics and thrombectomy heralded a refreshing dawn of a new era which changed this. The new catchphrase became "time is brain," and neurologists and nurses and other core team members answering to "code strokes" in the hospital symbolized the responsibilities of this new "clot busting" breed providers.

Still, it is all too often the case that despite expediency and effort, patients suffer the relentless blows of an embolism to a brain blood vessel, or a cruel degenerative disease which slowly wipes away memory, motor function, and the very words that we use to speak to one another.

Caregivers become just that: tireless laborers of love, tending to the most basic of human needs for those alive yet rendered incapacitated to care for themselves.

And as we learn more of its capacity for repair and recovery, this has brought new hope to the field. In this new light, it is worthwhile for us to come back to those germinal days of our early inspiration. In this collection of insights from healthcare professionals about their motivations for caring for patients, Dr. Kessarin Panichpisal encapsulated their words in an inspirational compendium which helps bring out the human side of healthcare workers.

Nazli Janjua. M.D.

Preface

I have been practicing medicine for more than 20 years, the last six of them as an interventional neurologist. Broadly speaking, I help patients who suffer from stroke, aneurysm, or other circulatory problems in their brain or spinal cord. Much the same as an interventional cardiologist inserts a stent to improve blood flow following a heart attack, I perform endovascular procedures for aneurysm treatment and treat strokes and help prevent them. Many of my patients have suffered acute ischemic strokes and find themselves at risk of more serious incidents unless proper blood flow is restored emergently. Seeing my patients regain motor function and return to their normal lives is the most rewarding part of my job.

As with any medical specialty, not every procedure succeeds. When things go wrong in my field, the consequences can be dire. Losing a patient changes a surgeon forever.

In my case, I found myself performing coil embolization on a patient's brain aneurysm. This involved placing a small catheter inside the aneurysm and filling it with platinum coils, some thinner than a human hair, which sealed the weakened artery after the catheter was removed. The procedure went well until the final step, when a small loop of one coil shifted and emerged from the aneurysm and into the healthy artery. This small loop was a big problem: a blood clot could easily form around it, precipitating a stroke. To fix it, I needed a stent, some extra hands, and moral support.

My senior partner, Dr. Thomas Wolfe, responded immediately to my call for assistance, and with his help I inserted the stent. Before I could push the metal coil back into place, it unspooled further and entered another artery. We added a second stent, but before we could position it, we needed to move the wire and catheter through the first stent. It proved impossible to move a wire that small into precise position, so I paused and performed an angiogram, which revealed devastating finding: active bleeding in the artery we had been working on, likely from the wire but possibly from part of the first stent. As the patient's bleeding worsened, we found ourselves using multiple coils to completely block the hemorrhaging artery. This was a pyrrhic victory. We stopped the bleeding, but at the unavoidable cost of a massive stroke.

Though I pulled myself together before breaking the news to her family, I could not hold back my tears during the most difficult conversation of my career. I relived each moment over and over, each time feeling more guilt and shame for not having anticipated a vanishingly rare sequence of events. The patient died a few days after the operation, and I cried for several days thereafter. I nearly quit medicine altogether.

On what might have been one of my last days as a physician, Dr. Wolfe walked with me down the hallway and encouraged me to stay on. He was a seasoned physician, and like any surgeon with much experience, he knew what I was going through. But his most effective words of wisdom had nothing to do with surgery itself. "Just because you fell off the horse," he said, "doesn't mean you need to sell the poor thing!"

Throughout the COVID-19 pandemic, frontline healthcare professionals have staked their lives and those of their families on caring for patients. That many lost the wager makes me appreciate my colleagues all the more.

Our jobs are difficult to begin with. Over the last two years, we have taken on the added burdens of risks to our health, of long-term sleep deprivation, and of a lack of balance between our working and personal lives. During the early days of quarantine in Milwaukee, I decided to reach out to fellow professionals throughout the healthcare field and learn how they coped with the pandemic. Questions swarmed my mind. Why do these healthcare heroes stay on the job? What gets them out of bed in the morning to face yet another long and grueling day? What got them interested in healthcare in the first place? If they could do it all over again, would they?

Before long, a bit of idle speculation grew into a compelling idea for a book. I began talking with colleagues past and present and sent out questionnaires under the project name *Don't Sell the Horse*. When asked whether they love their jobs, the professionals whose thoughts and experiences make up this book all answered, "Yes."

After receiving more than 200 completed questionnaires, I sat down and compiled them into this book. I hope you enjoy reading the first-hand reflections of healthcare heroes from across the industry. If you are one of us, please keep riding your horse. If you are considering a career in healthcare, I hope this book gives you some valuable insights from those who have already taken the plunge.

Kessarin Panichpisal, M.D.
Milwaukee, Wisconsin

CHAPTER 1

Administration

I 've been in healthcare for 13 years and have been the Manager of Advanced Heart Failure/Transplant for the past 6 years. I always had a calling to help people. Taking the advice of my mentor leader, I progressed into a management role starting from my ICU nursing role. If I were to do it again, I would still choose to be in healthcare but would have taken a more advanced clinical pathway to be more in direct patient care.

What drives me to keep going is recognizing that I have a responsibility to my patients and the people I serve. I am also motivated knowing I have an impact on how we provide care to our patients and the profound life event of a heart transplantation.

One of my most memorable experiences in my career is caring for an obtunded patient in the CVICU (Cardiovascular Intensive Care Unit) for more than two weeks. One morning, the patient woke up and I was able to share that joy with the patient's family and the other healthcare providers.

To me, it's important to remain sincere and honest with yourself. Don't pretend to be anything you're not. Trying to please everybody is impossible. If you did that, you'd end up in the middle with nobody liking you. You've just got to make the decision about what you think is best and do it.

~Adam Kallio, Manager –
Advanced Heart Failure/Transplant

Graduating from University of Wisconsin Milwaukee in 2016 is a very memorable experience for me. That's because I didn't like school at all, even though I did well in school. It took me longer to finish college than most because I took two year-long breaks. But I really pushed myself during my last year of college. I took winter and summer classes just so I could finish sooner and it was the best decision I ever made. I feel like I have opportunities now that I have a college degree.

I am now an Executive Assistant. Prior to that, I was an Administrative Assistant for three years. I started as a Clinical Office Assistant about five years ago and two years later, worked my way to becoming an Administrative Assistant. Throughout the five years I've been with Aurora St. Luke's Medical Center, I have always been with the Neuroscience Department.

I chose this job to grow in my career. It was a blessing that an opportunity to move up within the same department opened up for me. There are a lot of opportunities for many different positions when you work at a hospital. Even if you start out in a position that you may not like or may not see as the right fit for you, you can always move on to something else. I have also made a lot of connections and friends along the way. If I could go back in time, I would still choose this job.

"If it doesn't challenge you, it won't change you" is one of my favorite quotes. This is not an original quote but one that inspires me to go after what I want in life. I have worked very hard to get where I am today. I live on my own and just bought a condo about two years ago. My motivation is to keep working to be able to pay it off and pay for things that I want. I also like to travel so having something to look forward to motivates me to get up, go to work and make money so I can travel and have those experiences.

In my professional life, I have learned to be confident, to speak my mind and own up to my mistakes. I was very shy when I first started in 2015 as a Clinical Office Assistant. The longer I worked, the more I realized how important it is to share opinions because what you experience may not be the same as someone else's. Those ideas could help change your working environment for the better. Also, we are only human so we should own up to our mistakes and learn from them because it will only make us better both as a person and coworker.

~Anonymous, Executive Assistant

⟶⟩●⟨⟵

I think nursing is a wonderful field. Making a difference in the lives of others keeps me going. I think the only other job I would consider would be teaching, which was my parents' profession. To be honest, I chose nursing because I was told I would be good at it. My current leader suggested I consider a leadership role because he is confident that I would handle it well. I am truly enjoying this journey so far.

"Only those who will risk going too far will actually know how far one can go." This quote by T. S. Eliot really inspires me. I've also learned in my professional life to listen to everyone. The most memorable experience I've had in my career is meeting my wife in the same hospital unit.

~Bryan Kleinschmidt, RN,
Supervisor of Interventional Services

I've been a Manager of Clinic Operations for 3 years now. I would choose this job over and over again. I feel like I landed right where I should be. I love people. I love teaching, mentoring, and being a role model. I'm very passionate about supporting my team. I love to influence change in a positive, productive way.

The greatest lesson I've learned is to hold your head high and go into everything with a positive, confident attitude. It's mind over matter. If you are determined, anything can happen. It's really important to gather your network and meet as many people as you can. Resources are key in my leadership role.

When you can't control what's happening, challenge yourself to control the way you respond to the situation. That's where your power is. I will never forget that time when my clinic flooded with not only water, but fecal matter. It challenged me to think under pressure and come up with a quick plan. Clinics were re-routed to other spaces for the next four weeks and everything was a success.

My professional career started a little later in life, so I always say I went from "Mom to Me." My four children keep me going. I try to be the best role model for them. I'm determined to provide the best life for them and my professional life helps me to do that. Two of my children have muscular dystrophy and they push me to be the best person I can be. They deserve that.

~Courtney Sanchez,
Manager of Clinic Operations

I have had the pleasure of working with some very talented leaders and clinical staff in the Ambulatory Treatment Center and Pain. I had to fill some very big shoes when I came into this role. The previous leader, who was very well-liked and respected, worked side by side with them as clinical staff before becoming the lead. The team was very patient with me and gave me much needed support that helped me learn and grow as a leader. I have also seen significant growth in many of my team members over the past two years and I look forward to seeing where their paths take them in the future.

Being a Registered Nurse Lead afforded me a better work–life balance as a nurse with the benefit of maintaining a leadership role. As a leader, you can serve your team in ways that can empower them to "fix" what they know needs to be fixed. As a Clinical Nurse, you generally know that something could be done better but you may not have the tools nor the freedom to create the needed change. The Lead RN collaborates and partners with the Clinical Nurses to help them effect change. By listening to their concerns and ideas, helping them to look for alternatives, and giving them ongoing support, they are able to implement change together.

I am guided by this quote from John Quincy Adams: "If your actions inspire others to dream more, learn more, do more and become more, you are a leader." Making a difference in the lives of others motivates me. If I can't make a difference in the lives of the patients that we serve, then I derive satisfaction from making a difference in the lives of the Teams that I serve.

I also learned that you have to believe in yourself. Listen to that voice that tells you something is not right. Then do your research, put your argument together, and fight for it even though other, more powerful individuals may tell you that you are wrong.

Many years ago, I took care of a very sick man in the ICU. He would get a little better, get transferred out, but then come back to the ICU. He was in the ICU for many weeks. One night was particularly bad…he became septic (before we had evidence-based Sepsis bundles), got intubated, then started expelling copious clots around his ET tube. Despite sedation, he was aware of what was happening. He was very scared. Despite my hair trigger gag reflex (yes, I kept it together), I looked him in the eye and told him I would do everything I could to get him through it. I told him that I could see that he was a fighter. I reassured him that despite how scary things may seem, he could get better. I told him I've seen it before when another ICU patient, who was even sicker than him, got better after a few months. I told him how that same patient came back at Christmas with cookies that he baked for all of us. I said that I was looking forward to him bringing us cookies that upcoming Christmas. I think I saw him give a bit of a smile at that. Did I mention that he was Jewish?

All the Medical team members (It's never a good sign when you have many specialists on the case) had given up and wanted to discontinue his care. They felt his situation was hopeless but I disagreed. I found a physician who was willing to listen to me. I explained what a "fighter" our patient was. They just need to give him a little more time and to believe in him. After caring for him for many nights, I had the chance to get to really understand him. Only a nurse who has seen a patient through the ups and downs of a prolonged hospital stay can truly know a patient. He did get better. It just took time. By the way, he DID bring us cookies at Christmas and he baked them himself! I'll never forget him and the lessons he taught me.

~Deb K,
Registered Nurse Lead

I knew I wanted to be a nurse since I was six years old and I always felt like it would be perfect for me. I never thought I would have chosen a leadership track, but I feel like I am in a role that is a good fit. I like a good challenge, so I feel motivated to improve processes and break down barriers.

I've been a Manager of Patient Flow, House Supervisors, Bed Coordinators, and Tertiary Access Program (TAP) for 4.5 years. It feels as though this job chose me.

I had my first experience with patient placement and patient flow as a House Supervisor. I found that I enjoyed the "puzzle" of trying to find beds for all of our patients and coming up with creative ideas to make it all work. Later, that turned into the creation of my current role as volumes continued to increase at St. Luke's Medical Center.

In this profession, I have learned to never forget to connect with people on a personal level. No matter who you are working with or caring for, building relationships with others is an essential part of day-to-day work. Do not lose yourself in your "work."

I still remember the first patient that I ever had to transfer to the ICU. Knowing that I was able to advocate for their clinical changes and get them safely to the appropriate level of care was very impactful to me as a new nurse. I learned a lot that day and those lessons have stuck with me ever since.

My favorite quote is "Do unto others as you would have them do unto you."

~Leane Iglinski, Manager of Patient Flow,
House Supervisors, Bed Coordinators, and
Tertiary Access Program (TAP)

I find this job truly rewarding. I love my profession as a nurse and the ability to take care of people. Being in this role also allows me to care for my team members and support them in achieving their goals through mentorship, motivation, and empowerment.

My faith in God, my love for my family, my own personal drive and my passion for people are the reasons that motivate me to keep going!

Nurse leadership, I believe, is a sacred calling. Not everyone can be nurses and not everyone can be leaders. Throughout my 28 years as a nurse and in my 12 years in this leadership role, I have worked with a diverse group of people and built their trust. I have learned to respect different perspectives and keep a non-judgmental, open approach to varying opinions. I have learned to inspire people to feel joy and pride in our line of work. This profession has taught me to influence people to be their best and to find the power within them to make a difference in the patients' lives that we touch.

Leo Buscaglia once said, "Too often we underestimate the power of a touch, a smile. A kind word, a listening ear, an honest compliment, or the smallest act of caring, all of which have the potential to turn a life around."

At the young age of 21, I left the comforts of home to pursue my ambition and make a difference. I journeyed all the way to the USA to practice nursing. Being an only child, I know I caused my parents' heartbreak when I decided to explore life away from them. I traveled halfway around the world to a whole different country, not knowing a single soul, and with only $200 in my pocket. The only things I brought with me were my personal drive, courage, faith and hope!

I do believe that this opportunity is a divine gift and I have been very grateful for it. I would not have persevered if I had lack of faith. I was determined to follow my passion and desire to be a healer. My passion for nursing has opened many doors that helped me attain a leadership role. I couldn't ask for anything more rewarding than being able to help people and encourage them to live their passion.

I wish my story would also inspire my own children to live their dreams and be courageous. I want them to believe in the power of prayer to reach fulfillment in whatever goals they have set for themselves. I hope that my story uplifts and drives people to set high goals, test their limits, and persevere. I encourage them to keep going as they help people along the way. My advice: inspire, celebrate, and above all, believe.

~Leilani, Mazzone, Patient Care Manager

A note to the author:
Dr. Pan, it is a gift to have met you in my nursing career journey. You are an inspiration! Thank you for this opportunity to share my story. I wish you continued blessings and success. You are a beautiful gift to everyone and to the many lives you have touched. ~Leilani Mazzone

Perhaps the greatest feeling I ever had was feeling a pulse come back on an 18-year-old girl who was abandoned in a gas station parking lot. She had overdosed and was hypothermic. I was able to give her good chest compressions.

I've been a Support Supervisor/Team Lead in Medical Imaging for 1.5 yrs. Prior to this job position, I was a Computed Tomography (CT) Technologist for 16 years. I took this role because I'm unable to continue as a CT Technologist. If I could go back in time, I would have chosen to be a veterinarian or nurse. I feel limited in this role.

I am a fixer. If I have a problem or if someone asks me to fix it, I have to see it through. I also believe that you can learn something new every day. The first time you think you know everything is the day you will kill someone.

This is not original, but it makes me keep going:

Fate whispered, "You cannot withstand the storm."
I whispered back, "I am the storm."
That one reminds me to square my shoulders and face whatever it is, head on and not quit.

~Meaghan Neice, Support Supervisor/
Team Lead Medical Imaging

I have been the Nurse Manager of CVICU (Cardiovascular Intensive Care Unit) in Pomona Valley Hospital Medical Center (PVHMC) for 22 years and I managed Tele 3 station 2 and 3 (formerly Post Coronary Care Unit, along with CVICU) until 2008.

Initially, I did not want to be in a management role. But the acting head nurse asked me to cover for her while she took a leave of absence. When she left and the hospital re-organized, the staff asked me to apply for the job. I'm glad I did and the rest is history. Up to now some of the original staff still reports to me.

The greatest lessons I learned in my professional life are: to treat people the same way I wish to be treated; to be fair all the time; and to manage with my heart. The number of lives we save motivates me. Some patients would not have made it if it weren't for the treatment we provide. Our CVICU staff is excellent. They are very caring, competent, and compassionate. I am so fortunate to work with them. I also practice gratitude every morning and at night to keep me motivated.

One of my most memorable experiences while in this profession is when my husband Dan and I participated in the Pink Glove dance contest. We represented PVHMC and won first place. The other one was when my daughter Kristle surprised me by showing up in Boston as we were receiving our Beacon Award for Excellence from the American Association of Critical Care Nurses.

~Myrna (Mimi) Sarmiento, BSN, RN, CCRN
Nurse Manager, CVICU at Pomona
Valley Hospital Medical Center

I've been a Nurse Manager for the Illinois Division of Medical Cannabis for 3 years. I believe medical cannabis does improve the lives of patients living with debilitating medical conditions. I am so moved when a patient begins to cry while thanking me for giving them their life back. It makes me appreciate the part I play in helping them. Many patients have told me they had lost weight from depression brought about by their pain or other symptoms from their debilitating condition. They go on to tell me about how they were able to work again and function in a way they had not for years. My job is very rewarding.

I have selfish reasons for continuing to do what I do. It makes me feel needed. It gives me a sense of pride when I do good work and it makes me feel accomplished when I am able to help someone or comfort them in their time of need.

My nursing career of 37 years has been amazing— from working 22 years in the Emergency Department (ED) of a Level I Trauma Center to transferring to a State job. I would not choose any other profession. The colleagues I have met have become my lifelong friends. Best job in the world!

This profession has taught me to have compassion and empathy for all of mankind. Remember, you have not walked in their shoes. I learned that life is precious and not guaranteed. Hug your loved ones often.

Every day while working in the ED, I would pray, "God please don't let me hurt anyone today." We are all human and we make mistakes. Now my mistakes may only be on paper or on policy issues. In the ED, it could be with a patient. God never let me down.

In my career, I have two memorable experiences to share. The positive one was when I was nominated for an Illinois registered nurse award by a lovely couple that I met in the ED. The husband was sitting on the side of the stretcher when suddenly, while he was talking, he collapsed on the left side of the stretcher and became unconscious. His wife was horrified. In viewing the heart monitor, I noticed he was Bradycardic. I grabbed the atropine which was in a crash cart in the room, and pushed it intravenously. Then her husband slowly sat up on the stretcher, alert and talking. It was like a slow rewind of his slumping to his side. This story is why the wife nominated me. What I did was something any nurse would do. I did not receive the award which goes to registered nurses who make a difference behind the scenes by writing books, creating policies and/ or doing research— all of which are highly important in moving the nursing profession forward. The day I received notice that I was nominated was the day I found personal affirmation that I was right where I belonged.

The second one was heartbreaking. I received a six-year-old trauma patient who was hit by a school bus. What caused him to be hit is much less likely to happen today due to changes in safety policy. I think about that change often because this child may not have been hit, if only the preventive policy had already been in place. His mother was parked on the side of the road and let her child out. There was a school bus parked next to her in the street. The small child walked too close to the front of the bus for the bus driver to see him. Now they have arms in front of school buses. The child had a closed head injury and from the CT, had numerous areas of bleeding on his brain. While in CT he went into Pulseless Electrical Activity, so we started CPR. Unfortunately, the child passed away. I still remember everything but what I remember most is when I was comforting the devastated mother. All the while she kept repeating over and over, "He was talking to me while I was holding him in my arms after he was hit." We were both crying and holding each other. I will never forget the mother and her son.

~Paula Atteberry, Nurse Manager for the Illinois Division of Medical Cannabis

I'm the Senior Director of the Neuroscience Service Line. I have held this role for seven years but I have been working in Neuroscience Strategy and Development since 2006. I shadowed a neurosurgeon when I was considering medical school and although I ultimately chose a business career, I truly fell in love with Neuroscience. I really enjoy what I do. If given the opportunity to go back, I am not sure I would choose something else. However, if life had been written a different way and choices were endless, I may have chosen a path that included the care of animals in an entirely different profession and arena.

"She was powerful not because she wasn't scared but because she went on strongly, despite the fear." This quote by Atticus inspires me.

The greatest lesson I've learned is that in healthcare, it really does take the entire team. Despite physicians often being in the center of the spotlight, their delivery of care is not possible without the collective team of advanced practice clinicians, nurses, support staff, and administrative team. And although the intellectual expertise provided by physicians is paramount to patient care, often overlooked is how many steps there are to get a patient to the physician in the first place.

Changing people's lives is my motivator. Although I am not a clinical healthcare worker, I know that the work I do allows those clinical teams to deliver the needed care to so many patients.

My most memorable experience is the day I got to cut the ribbon on a brand new, stand-alone specialized Neuroscience Institute that I had designed from the ground up.

~Rachael Mahoney, Senior Director
– Neuroscience Service Line

I have been a Manager of Clinic Operations for a year, but have been working in healthcare for a total of 13 years.

I enjoy working with my team. I feel like I help make a difference by taking the pressures off the front-line team members, working on process improvements and education. I have worked in Aurora Neurosciences Innovation Institute for over six years and this group is truly one of the best I've ever worked with. Everyone is so passionate about their role in the patient care continuum and it is inspiring.

I never in a million years dreamed I'd work in healthcare! My husband convinced me to join the rescue squad "just to drive the ambulance." I quickly realized I wanted to help and become an EMT. I still didn't think I'd make a career in healthcare but the economic downturn during my college graduation year forced me to take a different path. I ended up working for a health system in the IT department. From that moment on, I realized I enjoyed healthcare and the operations end of it. And so, I started my journey in the healthcare profession. There are days I wonder if this is the right career for me but overall, I wouldn't trade it!

There are so many aspects to healthcare. Making what seem like small changes in workflows can have a much greater impact than you realize. Exploring all possible outcomes and challenges along the way before finalizing changes is very important.

My favorite quote that gives me inspiration is from Winston Churchill. "Success consists of going from failure to failure without a loss of enthusiasm."

Picking one most memorable moment isn't easy. I'd have to say the first time I was able to step into an OR and observe a case made a big impression on me. While a clinic manager certainly doesn't need to be in an OR, it truly opened my eyes to the inner workings of our team and the care continuum the patient goes through. It really made me appreciate healthcare in a whole new light.

~Shannon Clark, Manager of Clinic Operations

I'm the Director of Imaging Services. I have been in healthcare for 17 years doing both clinical and leadership positions. This is my 2nd career. I started off in business management, looking for a career and not just a job. I wanted a career working with and helping people— which is my passion. I landed a career in radiology services, which allows me to live out my passion of helping our patients live well and providing them with the care they need. I just wish I knew more about healthcare growing up. I may have chosen a career in medicine as a physician.

My family and most importantly, my patients motivate me to get up and keep going. Without these two, motivation would be hard and my purpose would be lost.

In this profession, I've learned to always try and be kind to everyone. People may not always remember your name but they will always remember how you made them feel through your actions.

My personal quote is "Do what you have to do, to do what you want to do." The meaning behind that quote is there are things that you really hate doing or want to push off, but they could be very important to getting you to where you need to be later.

One quote that has always stuck with me during my days as an athlete and in my clinical and professional career as well is: "Hard work beats talent when talent doesn't work hard" by Tim Notke.

I will never forget the time when I was working in the Emergency Department (ED) one weekend. A toddler came in unresponsive and not breathing. The entire ED team worked to save this patient. Every measure was taken and everyone pitched in with a sense of urgency— the ED physicians, nurses, imaging, and the ED techs. Although the outcome was not favorable, I will be forever touched by the gestures of kindness, compassion, relentlessness, and dedication that was given to that patient. As I still reflect on that moment, I know I made the right choice to be in healthcare to work with such caring individuals who always put the patients first.

~Sonnie Wilbert, Director of Imaging Services

I'll be an Administrative Assistant Senior for 18 years by September 2020. I chose this job as I was keenly aware of Advocate Aurora's outstanding reputation and I also am carrying on the legacy of my mother and father who are both 40+ year Leadership "veterans" with Aurora Health Care.

Given the chance to do it all over again, I would still choose this job. I started in a different field than where I am now, but I believe team members working within this ever-growing organization have a wonderful advantage. That is the ability to move into different career paths.

Knowing I am contributing to excellent patient care motivates me to keep going. In my professional life, I learned that you get out what you put in. You will be recognized for your hard work. My favorite quote is "Always assume positive intent."

Assisting clinical staff with "N95 mask fit testing" sessions during the pandemic made a big impact on me. They were able to perform the ever-increasing duty of caring for our patients without endangering their own lives.

~*Tammy Mueller, Administrative Assistant Senior*

CHAPTER 2

Anesthesia Technician

I love helping people. It is rewarding to be with patients before they are induced in preparation for surgery. Being there for them right before a procedure is the best feeling in the world. I know that the Lord has blessed me to be in this position.

I am an Anesthesia Technician and I have been doing this for about two years. I've also held a position in the Cardiovascular Intensive Care Unit (CVICU) for 23 years.

There is a quote by Pastor Marlon Lock that inspires me: "My today is better than my yesterday, and my tomorrow will be better than my today."

My most memorable experience in my career is being told that I was going to be a failure in this position. I was also called stupid but God and the strong support from my family and friends helped me get through orientation.

What keeps me going is the strength that God gives me every day to provide and serve patients as well as my coworkers. I am also motivated by being able to lead by example. The greatest lesson learned in my professional life is to never forget where you have come from. You never know when you would end up on the receiving side of the same situation.

~Shawonda Bezue,
Anesthesia Technician

CHAPTER 3

Art Therapists

All my life I've always been interested in art. It's been a passion of mine since I was a child. As a shy kid in high school, I started using my art class homework as a means of communicating emotions that were too complex or too overpowering to speak about. Deciding what I wanted to do in my future was like throwing puzzle pieces up in the air to see what happens. When I began looking into colleges to attend, I stumbled across one that offered an Art Therapy major. Learning about the field of Art Therapy was like watching all those puzzle pieces fall to earth and one by one align perfectly with one another. I couldn't believe there was actually a job built around helping other people express themselves using art as I had been doing all year. I was immediately struck with the realization that this is what I need to be doing with my life.

I am now an Art Therapist, specializing in medical oncology art therapy. I've been working in this position for a little over eight years.

There have been times where I think that other routes would have been easier. Growing up, I've only ever had one other plan for my life. If I had chosen that life path instead, it would have meant less schooling, less tests, less licensing fees, and possibly more job stability, but would I have been happy? Working in that other field for a few years earlier in my life tells me that I wouldn't have been happy there. I truly believe you have to have the passion for what you do. Without it is like beating your head against a wall every day. I do believe there is no other right path for my life than to be an Art Therapist.

I believe in the power of art. Art has the power to express emotions that are too complicated or difficult to translate into words. Art has the power to make people smile when they're having a bad day. Art can also trigger memories that have been long forgotten. It surpasses language barriers and brings people together. Art may not have power for everyone, but it can still accomplish amazing things.

The main motivator I have is watching the progress the patients are making. I've seen art help motivate the patient and keep their mind on their goals, rather than focusing on the hardships they've endured. I've watched art help patients, especially those who began closed up and angry with the world. Over time, they open up and share their burden thereby making them feel a little lighter and more trusting. Art has helped cancer patients come to terms with new diagnoses, better understand their relationship with the disease, and find ways to celebrate who they are as a person despite the diagnosis. Watching clients find ways to express themselves and keep going in the face of harsh difficulties sustains my motivation to continue doing this job. I am inspired when I see them believing in themselves.

"Trust the process" is a quote that my graduate school professors would hammer into our heads. We heard it so many times you would start to hate it because it's a difficult concept to figure out when you're just starting. It can be confusing to understand how to trust in the art process without experiencing it. At some point, it just starts to click. You have to trust your own intuition and you have to trust that the act of creating art will help bring out what needs to come to light. It may not always happen right away, but trust the process and it will emerge.

There was a woman who would come to the infusion clinics for her chemo treatment. This woman spoke primarily Spanish and very little English. I, on the other hand, speak primarily English and very little Spanish. The first day I met this woman, her daughter helped translate. The woman wasn't sure about participating in art because it was something she had never tried before. She seemed reluctant but willing to try the art process. I began to work with her every week when I saw her there. Sometimes her daughter was there to help translate, sometimes the woman was by herself and we had to wade through visual cues and short, poorly put together sentences consisting of languages that neither one of us was good at. After some time, this woman began to wave me over as soon as she saw me enter the clinic. She expressed through her daughter that she was starting to look forward to creating art during her chemo treatments. It helped her become more relaxed and happier while she was at the clinic. This was when I began to truly see the power that art holds. Although she and I could barely communicate, art broke through that language barrier. Art helped this woman look forward to her treatment rather than dread it. I remember her every time I meet someone new in the clinic, especially someone who doesn't speak the same language I do. We may not be able to easily talk to each other, but we can through art.

~Erin Hein, ATR-BC, LPC
Art Therapist

The opportunity to become an Art Therapist appeared when I was laid off from a technological job. I used my severance education package to follow my passion for art and creativity in combination with wanting to serve vulnerable populations. I've been working as an Art Therapist for 20 years now.

I am fortunate to be able to practice from my area of passion. I spent my first career in a position that paid well but did not serve my soul. Thankfully, as a second career, art therapy both serves me as a professional and contributes to the wellbeing of patients.

I have learned a few things in my professional life. First, personal contentment and meaning in life are fed by following a career path that accentuates personal strengths. Finding a way to maintain personal mental and physical health through the context of a professional job serves the entire community.

The profession of art therapy can be strenuous and at times grief and pain can complicate relationships with patients. It is imperative for Art Therapists (and other caregivers) to take care of themselves both within the profession, and within personal lifestyle in order to best serve patients, families and co-workers.

I think the variety and creativity, which are part of my job, keep me interested and engaged. We are constantly looking for better ways to serve patients, the community, and fellow caregivers. I find patient successes inspiring and love to be a background part of their healing. I also love to see the healing community grow. I enjoy talking about art therapy and presenting ways that it can be helpful across the medical system.

Carl Jung spoke of passing through the flames of passion and growth through life's challenges. This is similar to the story of the Black Madonna whose image survived the fire. The idea of walking through the flames as opposed to avoiding or circumventing struggles is something I live by, and something I share with patients as they face significant life challenges. I do believe that it is the response to challenges in life that define human character.

I have many memorable experiences in this career. Holding the space for a widow whose husband suddenly died is a big one. She said goodbye to him through a 6-week portrait painting session. Other clients have had similar experiences, but this one stands out specifically. Watching our art therapy program grow within the Advocate Aurora community is also a great experience. It feels good to be appreciated.

~Jill McNutt, Art Therapist

CHAPTER 4

Cardiac Procedure Technicians

I 've been a Cardiac Procedure Technician for two years. I like the challenge this job gives me. It's also because of the opportunity to learn new skills that I chose this job. I think that I would still choose to do this type of nursing if I were to go back in time. But I am open to different opportunities and learning new skills.

I would say that it is the idea of bettering myself and trying to make someone else's day a little bit better that pushes me to get up and keep going at this job. Audrey Hepburn once said, "As you grow older, you will discover that you have two hands: one for helping yourself, the other for helping others."

This job also taught me to treat the patient the way you would like your family member to be treated.

I've had some pretty memorable experiences, both funny and tough. The most memorable would be the passing of a patient in the oncology unit. The patient was someone I had worked with and formed a relationship with for some time. Seeing her pass away and no longer being in pain was cathartic for everyone who worked with her. It gave us solace to finally see her at peace.

~Christen Lambie,
Cardiac Procedure Technician

I originally applied for a nursing assistant position but this Cardiac Procedure Technician position was available. After shadowing the unit and a few phone calls, they offered me the job and of course, I said YES!

I have been a Cardiac Procedure Technician here at St Lukes Medical Center for almost four years. I would ABSOLUTELY choose this job over and over again. It's been the greatest experience and I'm always learning something new. If anything, this job motivates me to want to go back to school to become something more in this field.

Whether a patient smiles at you or not, or whether a patient treats you positively or negatively, there's truly no way of knowing what's happening in their life. For example, a patient could have recently been diagnosed with a certain sickness, could have lost a loved one, or could not meet their obligations due to hardships. Never judge a book by its cover.

When patients thank us for what we do or how we did something for them, that's motivating. I know I'm making a difference or an impact in a positive way.

My favorite quotes are: "I never lose. I either win or learn" and "Your life is as good as your mindset."

I make jokes on the daily with patients to distract them from intravenous lines and other possible painful things. Sometimes when they return, I remember what things worked for them the last time. I've had past patients come up to me and introduce themselves and thank me for taking care of them or a family member.

Awhile back we had a patient who was going in for a procedure to increase blood flow and decrease plaque buildup. After I put his IV, he proceeded to tell me to have a great Friday. I mentioned that I'd be there all day and most likely still see him after his procedure. Earlier in the conversation while putting in his IV, we had talked about everything from pets, life, to the weather and he had noticed that I was younger. He offered me some advice: "Think positive."

Later, something happened in the procedure room and that man didn't make it. I thought it ironic that I had a tattoo with those exact words. To this day, I think of that man and find the positivity in most of my day-to-day situations. Staying positive doesn't mean you have to be happy all the time. It means that even on hard days, you know that better ones are coming.

~Monica S., Cardiac Procedure Technician

CHAPTER 5

Certified Nursing Assistants

I'm a Certified Nursing Assistant, currently working at Cardiovascular Intensive Care Unit (CVICU). I've been in this position for seven years. I thought I wanted to be a nurse for my adult career. But if could go back in time, I would be a Real Estate agent.

In my professional life, I learned that good things do not come easily but my family and goals keep me going. I can do all things through Christ who strengthens me.

Helping care for the 1,000th heart transplant patient in the CVICU at Aurora St. Luke's Hospital is most memorable for me.

~Anonymous, Certified Nursing Assistant

I'm a Certified Nurse Assistant (CNA). As an immigrant, I wanted to build a career in healthcare. Upon the advice of my cousin, I took the CNA course as a stepping stone. What motivates me to get up and go is the feeling that I'm going to help or make someone's day better while they couldn't do it themselves. The greatest lesson I've learned in this job is to be patient, kind, and human.

Every day, I live by this quote: "Choose your attitude."

One of the most memorable experiences I've had was when we were tasked to help move a legacy patient at the OR after her condition started to go downhill. The patient was overweight and she was on a large bed. The respiratory staff had to climb on top of the hospital bed to help ventilate the patient with an Ambu bag. It was quite a scene that I still remember especially whenever I see that patient. Be dedicated to what you do.

~Charles Waithaka, Certified Nurse Assistant

I wanted to learn more about the brain and how it functions. That's how I ended up becoming a Certified Nursing Assistant. I've been a CNA for two years now in the Neuro ICU. I love bringing smiles and laughter to my patients. I would choose this job time and time again. If I didn't choose this job, I think I would want to work in the Emergency Department.

The Dalai Lama once said, "The purpose of our lives is to be happy." I believe in just living life to the fullest.

It is most rewarding when I see patients return to the unit and update us on their rehabilitation progress. I love seeing them dressed up in normal clothes instead of our fashionable green hospital gowns. Most of all, I love seeing patients walk. Working in Neuro ICU, I encounter a lot of patients who have had strokes and need rehab to regain all function and mobility.

The greatest lesson I've learned is to have compassion and empathy for patients. It is very fulfilling to comfort patients and monitor their progress firsthand instead of judging them.

~Mai Ger Vang, Certified Nursing Assistant

⸻ ⟫◆⟪ ⸻

I've been a Nursing Assistant for two and a half years. What inspired me to choose this career was what my grandma went through with her cancer and end of life condition. She had a hard time getting the proper care. It made me want to make a difference in someone's life for the better. I would choose this career over and over again.

I learned that every patient is different. The body language and bedside care are different for every patient. By learning this, I am able to care for my patients the proper way.

The patients that truly touch your heart and appreciate all the hard work you do are what motivate me. A lot of my patients on my floor come back to the hospital often so I am able to maintain a good relationship with them. They make you want to keep helping and keep going.

Nursing is a work of heart. My most memorable experience was when I cared for a patient who was having a horrible time. The staff couldn't figure out why she was bleeding. She had no appetite but craved lemon pie. I decided to pick one up for her and bring it in the next day during my shift. The light in her eyes and the smile on her face almost brought tears to my eyes. I would sit with her and talk as often as I could. Her family sent a long message on a card to my floor thanking me for all the time I spent with their mother. This just shows how little things can truly make a difference in a person's life.

~McKayla Spurlock, Certified Nursing Assistant

CHAPTER 6

Chaplain

I did not choose to be a Chaplain. This job chose me. It is something I was called to do. Henri Nouwen called chaplains "wounded healers." Our woundedness that we have suffered in our lives inspires us to accompany others in their journeys as a loving, respectful, listening, empathic, and compassionate presence. We tend to believe healing is holistic: involving body, mind, and spirit. We hope our presence nurtures emotional and/or spiritual healing that may impact the bodily outcome too. I first felt called to serve God when I was twelve while gazing at the stars. I felt the Spirit nudge my soul. At that point I had no idea I was called to chaplaincy, and it has been a long journey to get here.

I have been serving as a Chaplain for over six years. I would still choose this job if I were to start over. Serving as a Chaplain is a privilege. I learn so much from those I serve and am touched so deeply by them. It is such meaningful work. Vulnerable people open up to us and share the deepest parts of themselves: what is on their hearts and minds, what are their hopes and fears, what are their needs, and what resources might support their finding strength, peace, or resilience. It is very fulfilling to make a difference and have this purpose.

I also enjoy chaplaincy because it is ever-changing and active. You never know what the next moment may bring. Contrary to popular assumptions, most of our encounters have nothing to do with death, but instead with life and living. We provide emotional as well as spiritual support. Some desire traditional spiritual practices while others do not. That is okay. We serve everyone who needs a loving presence to be there with them. Chaplaincy is not a solitary role. We are part of the interdisciplinary care team, which I enjoy.

Perhaps the greatest lesson I've learned in my professional life is to be still and silent. It allows the person you are serving to guide the conversation and gives them space to think and get the courage they need to reveal what is in their heart and mind. Being still and silent helps me to respond, not react to the situation. For me, being still allows the Spirit to guide me. Serving the hurting and suffering, the joy and fulfillment in making a difference, and my call— these all continue to motivate me.

Three biblical scriptures inspire me:

a) "Be still; and know that I am God!" Psalm 46:10 NRSV
b) "You shall love the Lord your God with all your heart, and with all your soul, and with all your strength, and with all your mind; and your neighbor as yourself." Mark 12:30-31 ESV
c) "And what does the Lord require of you? To do justice, and to love kindness, and to walk humbly with your God?" Micah 6:8 NRSV

For me, it's all about love.

It is impossible to name one chaplaincy experience that made an impact on me. There are so many and varied experiences. Some of my most memorable include supporting the family of a young child who attempted suicide and ultimately recovered. Another was accompanying a woman who, after much resistance, ultimately decided to have the amputation she needed to live. She later became motivated to do her best in therapy and life. I also remember mediating a conflicted family who ultimately agreed on an end-of-life decision that was in line with the patient's wishes.

Other moments include helping a patient find peace in accepting open heart surgery; supporting a young mother with a brain tumor find the strength she wanted so she could live for her baby, providing sacred ritual for a patient and family which enabled hope and peace to arise as a patient died; and accompanying the family of an opioid overdose patient as they let him go. They grieved but ultimately found hope and joy through his heroic donation.

I recall advocating for a cancer patient who did not feel heard when she did not want to pursue aggressive chemotherapy and radiation as well as journeying with family members of a patient with a massive brain tumor as they made the decision to let him go. And of course, it's always special supporting other team members in their grief, stress, exhaustion, or despair and helping them find resilience, rest, hope, or peace.

~Rev. Kathleen Mahoney M.Div. BCC, Chaplain

CHAPTER 7

Clinical Office Assistants

" Promise me you'll always remember you're braver than you believe, stronger than you seem, and smarter than you think." ~Winnie The Pooh

I was close to my grandma who loved Winnie the Pooh and she always reminded me of this quote. She was sick for most of what I can remember, yet she was the strongest person I knew. She battled cancer for years. When it would come back, it would always come back worse. She never let it bother her, though. She always just kept going.

I had a rough childhood and my grandma was always the most stable person I had. My grandma and this quote became my inspiration and source of strength. I actually got "braver than you believe" tattooed on my arm. It's a great reminder when I'm having a rough day that even though my grandma isn't here anymore, I know she's watching over me every day.

I would like to say I "fell" into this job, or the job picked me. I never thought I would be working in health care; I always had an interest in childhood education and was working at a daycare. After I had my daughter, I realized that working in a daycare just was not working out, and it was time to look for more. I applied for a patient service position and started with Aurora at the RiverCenter location. Shortly after, I transferred to St. Luke's and joined the Neuroscience family.

I would pick this job a thousand times over, especially the neurology aspect of it. I, of course, would love to be able to grow within the department. The patients, providers, and staff are what make this job the best. We are like a family here. I have learned so much being here and have met some wonderful patients.

The greatest lesson I have learned is how important coworkers are. I would have never met my best friend if I didn't work where I am now. It's funny how things work. She and I used to work at the same place prior to working at Aurora, in different departments but we never even knew who each other were. I call my coworkers my "work family." I don't have the greatest/closest family so meeting the people here—sharing our laughs, hurts, and goofiness— makes me thankful for where I am. I never knew how grateful I would be to sit on the floor in a crowded office during lunch on my worst days. Just knowing that if I am in there with them, all the bad days turn into silly moments that I will forever cherish.

~Amber Ahlborn, Clinical Office Assistant

I'm a Clinical Office Assistant and I've been in this role for six years. I wanted a career where I was able to help people. Knowing I can make a different in a patient's life motivates me. I would definitely choose this job again if I were to go back in time.

"Be the change that you wish to see in the world." This quote by Mahatma Gandhi inspires me.

I will always remember the time when a family member of a patient thanked me for being kind and for taking the time to have meaningful conversations with the patient. Apparently, the patient wasn't usually treated that way.

In this profession, I've learned to work hard— whether it's for justice, health, or your professional career. The harder you work, the better you will be!

~Anonymous 1, Clinical Office Assistant

———————

I've been a Clinical Office Assistant for five years. This job allows me the flexibility to work with my school schedule. If I went back in time, I would still choose this job for that reason.

My mom is my greatest motivator. She has worked so hard for me. I would like for her to retire early and enjoy her life.

All the staff I have met at my current position also make this job worthwhile. Even if I have failed in my schooling, they have backed me up 100% and they keep pushing me.

These are the sayings that inspire me: "Keep smiling and keep pushing. Nothing comes overnight. You have the power to accomplish anything as long as you put your mind to it. Focus on your goals every day. You got this!"

The greatest lesson I have learned in this profession is that communication is key. If anything is bothering or you would like changed, you must speak up about it.

~Anonymous 2, Clinical Office Assistant

I am a Clinical Office Assistant and I have been in the medical field for 33 years. I started as a certified nursing assistant because I like helping people and interacting with the patients. Given the chance to it over again, I would still choose this field. I have seen some extraordinary outcomes and I have helped a lot of people over the years.

Everybody wakes up every day fighting a battle. Meeting them from a place of compassion, empathy, and kindness is imperative. When a person is dealing with something traumatic, they aren't themselves. They are very likely experiencing emotions they haven't had to deal with on such an intense level. It can be very therapeutic for them when they have someone listen with compassion and empathy. To them, it isn't about having the answers but about having someone be present with them, giving them care, compassion, and empathy.

I love seeing patients get better! Years ago, I worked at an inpatient rehab unit. I loved helping patients get stronger so they could discharge at their best. I loved watching the determination, strength, and resilience of patients that experienced a stroke or a limb amputation. I was fascinated to see them working hard to get back as much function as possible. Every year the rehab unit would have a reunion party for patients. It's wonderful to see them come back and visit us and specially to see how they were doing. It is one of my favorite days of the year.

"And the day came when the desire to remain the same was more painful than the risk to grow." I am not sure where this quote comes from but I heard it years ago and it stuck with me. This quote reminds me to not get stuck or stay in a rut. Instead, it pushes me to challenge myself to be the best I can be.

Here's a story about my most memorable experience I've had working in this position. I had just finished turning a patient named Mary L. I told her I would be back to check on her after helping the other residents eat lunch in the dining room. I was feeding another patient when I heard a voice say, "Go check on Mary."

I put down the plate of food I was holding and ran around the corner to her room. When I reached the doorway, I was stopped by an incredible sight. Radiating from the ceiling was a beautiful bright white light and it shined directly on her face. Her eyes were open and she had a huge smile on her face. She hadn't opened her eyes or smiled in several days.

I stood there totally enthralled. Then the light started to recede back into the ceiling. When it disappeared, I turned around and said to the charge nurse sitting at the nurses' station behind me, "Mary is gone."

She asked, "How do you know that? You're not even in the room."

"The light took her."

"What do you mean the light took her?" she asked as she walked around the desk.

I then told her about the light from the ceiling as we walked into the room together. She checked Mary with her stethoscope and confirmed she is gone.

I said, "I know. The light took her to heaven."

It was a very memorable moment and all these years later, I still remember it very vividly.

~Anonymous 3, Clinical Office Assistant

This job found its way to me. I knew someone who was a Clinical Office Assistant (COA) in the suite and she let me know that there was a job opening. I have been a COA now for one and a half years. I would absolutely make the same choice if I went back in time.

The greatest lesson I've learned in this field is that people are people. We all hold different roles but we all play an important part. I love that the doctors never looked down on us or acted as though they were better than anyone. Every single person in Aurora Neurosciences Innovation Institute (ANII) is kind, caring, and compassionate. ANII is truly a one-of-a-kind place.

I love to help people, to bring a smile on their faces even on days when it's hard for them to find a reason to smile. I have seen so many people on their journey with Neurosurgery. They were all so strong and determined to thrive. They weren't just patients. A lot of times, they felt like family or friends. I loved going to ANII each day because the people I work with are so amazing, making me feel I belong in this family.

These quotes inspire me:
"Not every day is good, but there is good in every day."
"Life is not about waiting for the storm to pass. It's about learning to dance in the rain."

I have so many memorable stories I could share but there would not be enough room in this book. But I'll never forget this one patient that I had seen in the waiting room on my first day on the job. I remember she was losing her hair. She was so fragile and thin. I remember her looking up at me. I smiled and she smiled back in return. As she came in for succeeding visits, we talked more and more. I was there through her journey— her surgery, her recovery and her follow-up visits. Seeing the light in her eyes as she smiled, even though she was going through so much, truly brightened my day as did so many other patients.

~Kymberly Drebus, Clinical Office Assistant

I simply enjoy helping others. I love the feeling you get when you know you have impacted a person or group of people. If I could go back in time, I would without a doubt choose this same job. I love my job as a Clinical Office Assistant and I have been doing this for two years.

I have learned in my life never to judge a book by its cover. There are many chapters in a person's life that we might not have read. It doesn't matter where you come from, how old or young you are, how rich or how poor you are. We all have a heart, we have feelings, we hurt, we love, we cry and laugh.

I guess what keeps me motivated and enables me to keep going is the fact that each day is a new chapter. You will never know how the day is going to end until you live it.

Facing life's challenges and knowing that you can make a difference in someone's life is an unexplainable feeling.

My most memorable experience in this job is meeting people on a daily basis. Most of these people have gone through tragic illnesses and health issues, yet they are so fortunate to be alive. Because of the work of the wonderful doctors that they are coming in to see, they are continuing to live. It is an honor to work for these healers who dedicate their time to saving lives.

~Maria Enriquez-Parada, Clinical Office Assistant

———⟫●⟪———

I'm a Clinical Office Assistant for the Neurology Department. I've been working here for two and a half years. I have always loved helping people and dreamed that one day I would have the opportunity to work at a hospital. I would have loved to go to college and become a nurse. I enjoy working with our doctors, nurses, and patients.

In my professional life, I've found that no matter what job or position you hold, a little kindness and a smile go a long way.

My family, my children, grandchildren and God are my motivation in life. By setting an example for my children, all things are possible.

Sometimes you will never know the value of a moment, until it becomes a memory.

~Olivia, Clinical Office Assistant

———⟫◆⟪———

I love helping people and being a Clinical Office Assistant fits my life. My daughter had been in physical therapy much of her younger years, so this job position is an ideal fit for me. I think if I could go back in time, I would go to school to become a nurse.

My job makes me get up and keep going. I know every day is going to be different. I get to meet new people every day and there's always something to do. This is my "Away Family."

This job has taught me that all people are created equal. I also keep this quote in mind: "To give of yourself doesn't cost anything."

The amount of people's lives I have touched will always leave an impression on me. I will never forget the thank you cards I received from patients' family members, thanking me for listening to their stories and making them feel important. They were, and still are, special to me.

~*Pennie Cialdini, Clinical Office Assistant*

CHAPTER 8

Coordinators

I'm a Business Operations Coordinator. I have worked in this role for almost 8 years, but I have worked at St. Luke's since I was 16. I started in the dietary department washing pots and pans and have worked my way up in different roles to the position I have now. I chose this job because I was ready for a change from my previous job and felt that this job would give me an opportunity to learn new things and grow professionally.

If I was able to go back in time, I would still choose this job. If I was unable to do this job I think I would like to do something where I am able to spend more time outdoors and not cooped up in a building.

In this profession, I have learned that you can only do what you can do. Some things are not under your control. All you can control is how you react to things. Try to stay positive and things will all work out.

My kids will always be my motivation. I want to be the best role model I can be for them.

Quotes that inspire me can change depending on what I have going on in my life at the time. A quote that has recently inspired me is the simple rule of life: "Do unto others as you would have them do unto you." My parents taught me this practice as a child, and I have always tried to live my life abiding by this rule.

Another quote that has helped me get through challenges would be: "Most of your stress comes from the way you respond, not how life really is. Look for the good, the lesson, and grow from it."

And finally, one more quote that has gotten me through some recent tough times is, "You are so hard on yourself. But remember, everybody has a chapter they do not read out loud. Take a moment. Sit back. Marvel at your life: at the mistakes that gave you wisdom, at the suffering that gave you strength. Despite everything, you still move forward. Be proud of this. Continue to endure. Continue to persevere. And remember, no matter how dark it gets, the sun will rise again."

One of my most memorable experiences in my career is working in healthcare. We were asked to watch a video called "The Heart of Compassion." In this video they showed different people in different scenarios. The video's theme was: What would you do if you could stand in someone else's shoes, see what they see, and feel what they feel? Would you treat them differently? This video touched me so deeply at that time. It made me look at people differently and try to put myself in their shoes. None of us know what anybody is going through personally at any given time. We need to have compassion for others! I am thankful that we were asked to watch this video. It has changed my life.

~*Jessica Haas, Business Operations Coordinator*

I've been an Interventional Radiology Coordinator for 30 years. I love taking care of patients and the type of cases I encounter in this department. If I could go back in time, I'd probably be a history teacher.

Patience is the greatest lesson I've learned in this profession. Providing for my family and helping people keeps me motivated to get up and keep going.

This quote from Winston Churchill inspires me: "We make a living by what we get, but we make a life by what we give."

I've had too many memorable experiences in this career to choose only one to share. Witnessing positive outcomes definitely is at the top of the list.

~Michael Farrell,
Interventional Radiology Coordinator

———⟫◆⟪———

I'm an Interventional Radiology Coordinator and have been doing this job for 4.5 years. I was in the food industry prior to this job but was looking for something more serious and fulfilling. A friend that works in the department suggested I apply for an Imaging Assistant role. After working as an interventional radiology coordinator for 3 years I was promoted into the coordinator role. I chose this job out of pure curiosity and a desire to help my fellow humans.

I love my job. Though it may be stressful and taxing at many times of the day, I love what I do. I love that throughout the day, I am able to reach people and help them.

The greatest lesson I have learned is to not give your absolute all into your job. You are still a person outside of your job and have basic needs. Those needs are important to meet just as much as the expectations that your job has for you.

My home life, personal desires and goals inspire me to wake up every morning and to keep putting one foot in front of the other. Without desires and goals, you have nothing to live for. It is important to set expectations and bars for yourself to meet. Otherwise, no one else will.

I don't live by one quote. I try to continue learning every day from different educators. I like to research different people in history every now and then to see how they inspired others. I then learn from their success to help better myself.

I would say the closest thing to a personal quote that inspires me is this: "Don't keep just one stick burning in one fire. It's good to have multiple fires burning with your stick burning in each of them." I'm not sure where I first heard this or who told me first, but it has been something that has stuck with me over the years, through school and my professional life. It has helped me climb the ladder at every job I have had and I will continue to use it in my life. My interpretation of this quote is that it is best to keep yourself well-versed not just in one thing but in multiple things. Keep your stick burning or keep your life active in many things. I believe this keeps more doors open for you and can lead you to have more opportunities in life.

I believe I am currently in the most memorable years of my career. I am surrounded by supportive and positive staff members. I love what I do and I am continually learning more and more each day. My job keeps me interested and I challenge myself everyday. I continue to enjoy helping the people I work with daily and I don't think it could get much better than this.

~Natalie A. Trejo, Interventional Radiology Coordinator

CHAPTER 9

Dentists

I tell people all the time that my field fits me to a T. I would absolutely choose this profession again if I had to do things over. I've been an Endodontist and practice owner for 22 years.

I decided to take up Dentistry because I wanted to find a way to help people in a professional way using my hands, mind, and compassion. Once I was in Dentistry, I realized that it is quite a wide-ranging field. I needed to find a way to focus. I chose to specialize in Endodontics (root canals). In Endodontics, a person can become an expert while helping patients get through a process that they may find terrifying.

I am not my work. In root canals, you get to grade yourself via x-rays on everything you do. I have learned that I am just human and not everything I do will be perfect. Doing the best you can do under whatever the circumstances is the goal. Perfection is not.

What motivates me is working with people, developing myself and others to function together. My goals used to be focused on dollar signs. Now, I am more intentional with the processes behind the actual dentistry.

I believe in the saying: "You have to take care of yourself to be any good to anyone else." As told to me by a life coach, "The problem is not the problem." When you dig down deeper, you discover your underlying insecurities beneath the problems or arguments you have.

After 17 years in practice without a mentor, I employed a coach and with his guidance I have found confidence and freedom. By humbling myself to the point of seeking help, I came to terms with my own vulnerability. With the newfound acceptance that vulnerability can be a positive experience, I opened up myself to other coaching opportunities and mentoring situations. This has truly been transformative in my personal as well as professional life.

~Gerald J Gray, DDS, MS
Dentist

I've been a dentist for more than 24 years. I chose this career because I come from a family of dentists. If I were to go back in time, I would still choose to be a dentist because I have been able to carve out a special niche in my life based on my dental choice. It has helped me to become very successful.

The greatest lesson I have learned is to surround myself with forward-moving people and those who recognize my mission.

I am motivated by caring for my patients and treating them with their dental issues. Dentistry comes easy for me and I enjoy every aspect of it. It has also provided me with a very comfortable life.

My motto and my personal quote is: "Money don't sleep."

Every day is a new experience. That is what keeps the machine going and life interesting.

~Glenn L. Gequillana,DDS
Dentist

CHAPTER 10

Emergent Medical Technician

I 've been a Licensed Practical Nurse or LPN for 30 years and I have been an

Emergent Medical Technician or EMT for 22 years. I enjoy helping people in need. It gives me the feeling that I've accomplished something worthwhile at the end of the day.

The only thing I would do differently is further my education so I could do more. Knowing that patients need my help and depend on me keeps me going.

Put others ahead of you. Listen to other people first. Their problems are more important than yours, and they need someone to listen to them, allowing them to release or express their emotions. This is what I've learned being in this job over the years.

My mother told me, "When you think that you are not good at anything, remember there is always something you can do better than anyone else— even if it's just tying your shoes."

The most memorable moment for me would be our annual fundraiser for the ambulance service. We always have a huge Christmas tree on Main Street. It was called the Tree of Love and it's decorated with lights and red ribbons. People would donate a white light in memory of a loved one or a colored light in honor of someone. We would put their names in a book. A pastor would say a few words, we would sing carols and then go to the fireball for cookies and cider. The whole town would turn up.

~Anonymous,
Emergent Medical Technician and
Licensed Practical Nurse

CHAPTER 11

Environmental Services

I have been working with Environmental Services (EVS) for about 2 years. I enjoy playing a big part in helping keep the environment clean and safe for everyone.

I would definitely choose to take this position again. I have learned how important it is to have EVS positions around. Knowing that I have an important job inspires me to keep going.

"For every dark night, there's a brighter day." I live by this quote.
All the kindness and appreciation I receive daily for my hard work makes this job so worthwhile.

~Katrina Windle, Environmental Services (EVS)

I work in Environmental Services (EVS). I lost my husband and needed a job, so I applied for this position.

I love what I do. In this job, I've learned to listen and help. I am greatly motivated knowing that we in EVS are needed.

The Digital Vascular Imaging (DVI) department is awesome. What is most memorable to me is how the team in Interventional Radiology and doctors treat me well.

~Lorena Lund, Environmental Services (EVS)

———⟫◆⟪———

I've been in Housekeeping for seven years now. I needed a job right after high school so I could pay for my college tuition since my family's financial situation was not good. I applied for many jobs but wasn't accepted because I didn't have experience nor a college degree. The company that I work for now doesn't care if I have no experience nor a degree.

If I were to go back in time, I'd still choose this job. It taught me how to humanely and professionally care about someone even if that person is not of the same race, doesn't have the same skin color, or doesn't speak the same language as me.

This is the greatest lesson I've learned in this job: No matter how many people look down on you because you clean someone else's mess, it does not define who you are as a person and what you truly believe in.

What motivates me to get up and keep going is my faith in God and my mother. They play a really important role in my life. Without them, I think I would not survive this cruel world where people try to define who you are or what you are going to become just by the type of work you do or your financial situation.

There's a verse in the Bible that always inspires me to move forward no matter how hard it gets:

> "Anyone who is among the living has
> hope. Even a live dog is better off than a
> dead lion." ~Ecclesiastes 9:4 NIV

I will always remember having a conversation with a cancer patient who was having suicidal thoughts. I still remember that day as if it was today because I was able to see that sometimes not even doctors can save your life. It opened my eyes to see that sometimes no matter how strong our faith is or how high our hopes are, our minds can make us doubt what we had believed our entire life. It's times when we feel like there is no light at the end of the tunnel.

After our conversation, she thanked me for listening to her and for giving her advice on why she needed to continue to live. That means a lot to me because she would have killed herself that day. Knowing I was able to stop someone from taking her own life just by listening to her and talking to her, made me realize that there's so many out there like her. There are people who just need someone to listen to their worries without being judged.

~Zoby, Environmental Services (EVS)

CHAPTER 12

Financial Advocate

M y job title is Financial Advocate and I have been doing this job for almost three years. I love to help others and this job is very rewarding. Seeing the patient's reaction when being told that their bill will be covered at 100% is the best feeling.

This profession has taught me to never give up. The love I have for my children and my life in general is what gets me up and keeps me going.

I live by these Principles of Reiki By Mikao Usui

Just For Today:

- Do not be angry
- Do not worry

- Be grateful
- Work with diligence
- Be kind to others

There was a time when a patient needed to establish a payment plan and did not know about financial assistance programs. After assessment, I realized the patient was eligible for 100% discount. The look on his face— when I informed him about it— was priceless.

~Laura Garcia, Financial Advocate

CHAPTER 13

Health Unit Coordinators

I've been a Health Unit Coordinator at St. Luke's Medical Center for 39 years. I like both the administrative part and the medical part of the job. I've learned in this profession that nothing stays the same and that things can change so much.

My family is my biggest motivation. What is most memorable for me is having repeat visitors tell me how comfortable they feel.

~Anonymous, Health Unit Coordinator

I am a Health Unit Coordinator (HUC). I have been in my current role since circa 2003, but I've been with the company since 1999.

I started my healthcare career as a nursing assistant. I knew that I wanted to be in healthcare because of my love for helping people. I truly enjoy helping and making a difference. I transitioned from a nursing assistant to a health unit coordinator.

Yes, absolutely! I would definitely choose this job again if I were to go back in time. Very early in my career, I reduced my hours as an HUC to work another job. After about a year, I went back to being an HUC full time. At that moment, I realized how much I truly loved being an HUC. I missed it more than I expected.

Things can get stressful at this job. It is all about how you deal and cope with that stress. It's not worth letting it stress you out. Stay positive. Remember, things will get better. It's ok to ask for help. We are all in this as a team! Also, be kind. You never know what someone else may be going through.

Knowing that I am making a difference by helping others motivates me and keeps me moving forward. Being able to help others truly fills my heart with joy.

I find this quote Catherine Pulsifer very inspirational: "Small acts of kindness can make a difference in other peoples' lives more than we can imagine."

~Christine D., Health Unit Coordinator

———⟫◆⟪———

I've been a Health Unit Coordinator for three years. I'm passionate about my job and helping patients with their every need. I love my job but if I were to go back in time, I would maybe consider being a lawyer.

I have learned a few great lessons in this profession. One is to make connecting with others a priority. The other is to always look on the bright side. Another is to focus on developing and utilizing your strengths.

My family is what keeps me going. I believe in the saying, "When you focus on the good, the good gets better."

When patients are happy and you know you put a smile on their face makes this job so rewarding.

~Jessica Janasik, Health Unit Coordinator

The very first HUC certification test was given in Phoenix, AZ. I was one of the first 1000 people to get certified. So, when I moved to Milwaukee from AZ. I applied at St Lukes in 1998 and was hired that day! I'm a Health Unit Coordinator and I've been doing this job for more than 22 years.

Would I choose a different career path if I were to go back in time? I am a big animal lover, and I would really love to work with animals in some capacity.

This job has taught me patience, but I am still learning! GOD is my motivator.

"The grass is not greener on the other side....the grass is greener where you water it." That's my favorite quote.

I was awarded the very last "Golden Sneaker" and my picture was presented in the lobby. That was a memorable moment for me.

~Mary Ann Rundle, Health Unit Coordinator

I am a Health Unit Coordinator (HUC). I have been an HUC for four years.

I chose this job after working 12 years as a nursing assistant. Healthcare has always been my passion and I was interested in working on the administrative side of healthcare.

Although my job is more administrative than hands-on with patients, I feel that working in the Neuroscience ICU gave me insight on nursing and motivated me to advance my career to become a registered nurse.

The greatest lesson I have learned in my professional life is that there is always room and opportunity to learn more. Learning never ends. Sometimes learning new things can be scary and uncomfortable. If I never got out of my comfort zone, I would not be graduating in less than five months with my associate degree in nursing (ADN)— which is a very rewarding career.

My motivation to keep going is very personal. Everything I do is for my children. I love helping people and I love my place of employment. The help and support of my family and work family have influenced my decisions and play a big part in my success.

A quote that really inspires and motivates me is the saying, "You only fail if you quit."

The most memorable experiences in my career almost always come from my patients and their families. Working in healthcare is very rewarding whether you work directly with patients or just greet them with a smile at the door. It costs nothing to be kind. I've had many patients and their families show appreciation and acknowledgment towards my services. It is an awesome feeling to know I have impacted people's lives in a positive way.

~*Natasha Green, Health Unit Coordinator*

After going to nursing school and obtaining my license, I knew it was not the job for me. But I like the energy of a hospital and am good at the administrative side of things.

I have been a Health Unit Coordinator for six years. This is my "4th" career. I have previously been in the financial world and interior landscape design. I'd love to run an estate sale business.

Perhaps the greatest lesson I have learned in my professional life is keeping an open mind.

There are so many people less fortunate than me who can't even do the simplest things. I am grateful for every day that I can get up, keep going on my own two feet, and contribute in some way to society. That's what motivates me.

I keep in mind two quotes that help me at work: (1) My Dad has always impressed upon me: "Never be late;" and (2) "There is one in every office": in response to my complaining about a coworker.

My most memorable moment was when 40 family members threatened me because I would not let them on the unit to visit a patient. The patient had bed bugs.

~Sara Dorr, 2L Neuro ICU
Health Unit Coordinator

CHAPTER 14

Licensed Practical Nurse

Prior to my current role, I was a Dialysis Technician for five years. One day, a nephrologist pulled me aside and said, "Tell me something, why aren't you a nurse?

I replied to him, "I'm working on it! I'm in nursing school."

He said, "Wonderful!"

This motivated me, especially coming from someone with so much expertise.

I've been a Licensed Practical Nurse (LPN) now for two years. I am currently in nursing school pursuing my RN degree. Making the decision to take my PN nursing boards and begin working as an LPN has given me added valuable experience.

Yes, I would absolutely choose this position again. It has been eight months that I have been in neuroscience. I've learned so much. I love it.

This greatest lesson I've learned in this job is that when you give your BEST, you have given ENOUGH.

This quote by Saint Francis of Assisi is one of my favorites: "For it is in giving that we receive."

I live a spiritual life and my perspective on life reflects that. As I continue to grow into my purpose, I get up every day thankful that I am able to continue to work towards my goals.

~Toni Bates, Licensed Practical Nurse

CHAPTER 15

Medical Assistants

I'm a Registered Medical Assistant and I've been in this position for almost seven years.

I was previously a Certified Nursing Assistant for 12 years and my body was feeling the aches and pains from the physical lifting and constant running around. I wanted to stay in healthcare but I felt I have never been book smart enough. Being a Registered Nurse (RN) just wasn't what I wanted either, so medical assistant was the next best job. Plus, by working in a clinic setting, I don't work weekends or holidays. I work normal hours from 8:00 am - 4:30 pm. That is why I chose this job.

Of course, I would still choose this job if I could go back in time. I've been in healthcare in general since I was 16 years old. I couldn't see myself doing anything else other than being in healthcare.

Complaining and doing nothing will get you nowhere, but action and participation will have good results. This is the greatest lesson I've learned on this job.

Providing for my family is a big motivator and keeps me going, but helping others gives me a purpose in life.

I'm inspired by the saying: "Every day is a journey, and we have our own path that we travel at different paces. No one is perfect, but we can try for perfection."

I feel every day is memorable. Every day I learn something new that has helped to become a better Medical Assistant and a better person.

~Anonymous, Medical Assistant

I was a senior in high school when I was offered to join a program through Alveno College and become a Certified Nurse Assistant (CNA). I then became a CNA and started working at a nursing home. One day I came to Saint Luke's Hospital to visit my grandfather. An MD asked if I could translate for him and if I had any medical knowledge. I notified the MD that I worked as a CNA and that I was happy to interpret. Once the interpretation was over, the MD gave me his business card, asked me to call his office and speak to his manager. He wanted me to say that I was being referred by the MD. I then became part of that MD team and attended Medical Assistant school at Milwaukee Area Technical College (MATC).

I have been a Medical Assistant for 13 years. Working in the medical field has taught me that life is too short to not enjoy it. As humans we want everything to go our way without thinking that a medical diagnosis can change your life completely. So I have learned to be thankful and grateful for what comes across my path in life. I still would choose this job if I were to go back in time. I enjoy everything I do, and I have learned so much.

My two daughters are my motivation. I want them to inherit my hardworking skills along with the reward of helping people in need. I have no personal quotes that have inspired me. My daughters are my inspiration to work hard. I want to teach them that nothing is impossible in life.

The most memorable experience I've had in this career is when I helped a patient obtain her costly medication approved by her insurance. It took me almost one year to do it. I was constantly on the phone.

~Araseli Ramirez, Medical Assistant

My job title is Medical Assistant. I have been actively doing this for two years. I am a people person. I love helping and being able to help others when they are not feeling their best. Yes, this is the job I would choose if I were to do things all over again.

Teamwork and good communication are the keys to a great work environment. This is the greatest lesson that this profession has taught me.

What keeps me going? It's knowing that I can make a difference in someone's day, that I am part of a great work family, and seeing the smiles on the patients face when they leave happy.

This is a quote that inspires me: "Keep smiling, and live your life. Tomorrow is not promised."

Getting hired to work as a Medical Assistant is one of my most memorable moments.

~Yolonda Cooper, Medical Assistant

CHAPTER 16

Medical Scribes

I am a Medical Scribe. This is a new position for me, but I have been in the healthcare field for about nine years as a medical assistant and I don't regret it one bit. I chose this job because it is a new challenge for me. If I were to go back in time, given my circumstances, I'd choose this job again. If I weren't a Medical Scribe, I'd probably be an EMT.

One of the greatest lessons I've learned in my professional career is that everyone yearns for compassion and empathy regardless of how they appear on the outside.

What motivates me is knowing and accepting that I have not yet accomplished my life-long goal of becoming a doctor. However, being surrounded by intelligent and amazing doctors everyday helps me tailor my personal values and principles for the next steps in my healthcare journey.

One quote that inspires me is, "It doesn't matter how long it takes to reach your goals. The time is going to pass by either way." Since hearing this quote, I have released so much pressure and anxiety within me.

My most memorable career experience is being recognized for having a good heart and genuinely caring about patients.

~*Sendi Becerra, Medical Scribe*

I am a Medical Scribe in cardiovascular clinics. I have been working at Aurora St. Luke's for a year. I chose this job as a stepping stone to getting into medical school. It allows me to be challenged and gives me a chance to see patients on the clinical side. If I could go back in time, I would still choose this job. I truly enjoy this job and the team I work with.

The greatest lesson I've learned from my professional life is that your adversity and experiences make you who you are. The right company will want you. The ones that don't are not the right fit for you.

I'm a child of first-generation immigrants. Knowing the struggles my parents have gone through is the motivation that keeps me pushing to become the best version of myself.

"Adversity introduces a man to himself." This quote from Albert Einstein serves as my inspiration.

My most memorable experience is when I was able to shadow a procedure.

~Sheesher Moua, Medical Scribe

My personal quote is: "I want to be capable, willing and ready."

My most memorable experience was when I began to prepare my work ahead of time, shortly after being assigned the scribe role. I was new to the job. I am a Medical Scribe in Cardiovascular clinics. I have been here for eight months. I chose this job for a pay upgrade and to challenge myself.

If I could go back in time, I would still choose this job. If I wasn't working in this place, I would focus on college and would be working at a restaurant most likely.

The greatest lesson that I've learned is that people may come from different backgrounds, cultures, and educational levels, but clinic culture and expectations always remain the same.

God motivates me to get up, be strong and keep going in life.

~Yasmine Lopez, Medical Scribe

CHAPTER 18

Nurse Practitioners

I'm a Stroke Nurse Practitioner. I have been a Nurse Practitioner for five years and a Registered Nurse for 13 years.

I became a nurse because of my passion to help people in need and my love of the human body anatomy/physiology. My first job was in a Neuro ICU and that is where I learned to love and appreciate neuro patients and neuro critical care. Because of this, I pursued a job in Neurology when I became a Nurse Practitioner.

If I wasn't a healthcare provider, I would own a bakery. Baking cakes, cupcakes, cookies, and desserts is my favorite hobby! The joy that my baked goods brings to others makes my heart happy.

Working in a hospital, I've learned that life truly is precious... so live each day to the fullest and spend all the time you can with your family, friends, and loved ones. You never know what tomorrow will bring.

What keeps me going is the fact that my amazing team saves lives and we protect people from major disability every day (and my paycheck)!

This has been a favorite quote of mine since I was a teenager:

> "Life may not be the party we hoped
> for... but while we're here, we may as well
> dance."

Being invited to speak at the International Stroke Conference in Hawaii is my most memorable experience in this profession.

~Amy Pesch, Nurse Practitioner

Learning keeps me going. The more there is to learn about a subject, the more satisfying it is to implement into practice.

I believe that thoughts become things. Of course, you need to put your thoughts into action but accomplishment always starts with a great thought!

I've been a Neurosurgery Nurse Practitioner for three years. I enjoy complexity and the opportunity to continuously learn. Some days are difficult but I appreciate those challenges after the fact. In this profession, persistency was key to my success.

My most memorable experience is being thanked by a patient for providing them with a warm blanket. I saw how grateful the patient was and realized some of the smallest actions can make the biggest difference. I consistently think about that moment and how I can make everyone's day a little bit more manageable.

~Anonymous 1, Nurse Practitioner

The thought that I am contributing positively towards someone's care motivates me. I want patients to have the best care possible and best outcomes.

I've been a Nurse Practitioner for six years. I chose this career because I wanted something challenging but rewarding. I like to be pushed. I loved being a nurse but I wanted more autonomy. I probably would still do the same job if I were to go back in time. However, it can be pretty taxing to be in this position.

I have learned in this profession that you can rely on more than just books to practice. Evidence and Evidence-Based Practice (EBP) are essential. I also learned to always be an advocate for the patient.

Here's an original quote: "Try not to suck [at your job]."

I have had many memories that are pretty incredible. Seeing a neuro critical care intensivist diagnose CJD over the phone was one of the most incredible things I've ever seen. For me, the most memorable experiences are ones in which the patients have the best outcomes.

~*Anonymous 2, Nurse Practitioner*

I'll always remember the patient who thought his life was over because he felt no one could fix him. To see him leave the hospital with a new lease on life made me realize anything is possible if you keep trying.

I am currently a Surgical Nurse Practitioner. I've been a Nurse Practitioner for seven years. Prior to that I was a Registered Nurse for five years.

For more than 10 years, I was a paramedic but decided to further my education. After becoming a nurse and working in the Surgical ICU, I wanted to again further my education. I then went to grad school for my adult gerontological acute care nurse practitioner degree. I love my job but if I could go back, I might try to go further with my education and perhaps go to medical school.

First and foremost, my family keeps me going. Next to them is enjoying my work and loving the people with whom I work closely.

You can't please everyone. That's the greatest lesson I've learned in my professional life.

I always enjoyed this quote:

"Watch your thoughts, they become words;
watch your words, they become actions;
watch your actions, they become habits;
watch your habits, they become character;
watch your character, for it becomes your destiny."

~Anonymous 3, Nurse Practitioner

I've been a Nurse Practitioner for a year. I love being a nurse but I wanted more autonomy. I would definitely choose this job again if I were to go back in time.

The greatest lesson I've learned in my professional life is to always be an advocate for the patient. Wanting patients to have the best care possible and best outcomes - that's what motivates me to keep going in this job. My most memorable experiences are ones in which the patients have the best outcomes.

~Anonymous 4, Nurse Practitioner

I most recently switched to becoming a Nurse Practitioner, but for the last seven years I was a Registered Nurse. My mother is a nurse, so I knew from a young age that I wanted to pursue this field.

I do love my job and I would still go into the medical field if I were to go back in time. But I probably would have gotten more schooling at a younger age. Looking back, I would have liked to do pharmacy, or anesthesia.

I have read this quote in numerous places and have always loved it: "Positivity always wins!" What this profession has taught me is that the health of people is really in their own hands. What keeps me motivated are the patients that sincerely say thank you and my amazing coworkers.

I'm not sure I have just one memorable experience to share. I just love helping others! That includes patients, their families, and other coworkers and staff. One particular memory that stands out is when we saved a man's life. Weeks later, he visited the hospital and the staff that saved him. To say the experience was absolutely heartwarming wouldn't be enough.

~Brittany Schoenick, RN, MSN, FNP
Nurse Practitioner

For almost three years now, I've been a Neuro-interventional Radiology (NIR) Nurse Practitioner (NP). When I was in my NP school clinicals, I observed a mechanical thrombectomy for acute stroke and was amazed that this intervention was possible for strokes. I also felt the team had a really good dynamic between the RNs, NPs, and MDs. That made me choose to pursue this career.

In this profession, I've learned that you must do your best in doing the right thing for the patient— even when you aren't sure or even when you're scared.

Mother Teresa once said, "We cannot all do great things. But we can do small things with great love." As a nurse I always thought about this whether it was feeding patients their pills individually in applesauce, putting lotion on their feet, or talking about something unrelated to their illness to distract them. The small things we do add up.

My most memorable experience so far was caring for a patient when I was brand new to the NIR team as an NP. She was an aneurysmal subarachnoid hemorrhage patient with a very long critical care course. On multiple occasions, she took a turn for the worse and we were unsure she would survive or even survive with any quality of life. I saw her countless times in her stay and wondered how she would do in the long term. Would she be able to return home to her teenage sons? Would she work again? Would she be able to eat and drink again? She was hospitalized for almost four months and went to a brain injury rehab center.

She returned about 6 months later for a repeat procedure and had made significant physical and cognitive recovery, almost back to her pre-aneurysm rupture baseline. She had no memory of being in the hospital for a prolonged period of time and no memory of the care we provided. She was smiling, happy, and healthy. It was so amazing to see her survive and recover.

My patients and my team push me to get up and keep going. I know our patients need amazing care and I always come into work knowing my team is focused on the patient. I would choose this job again, given the chance. I love my neuro patients and the amount of care and teaching I am able to provide in my role. I love my team and how we interact with each other to provide care. My team knows the only other job I would do is start a bakery so they are regularly spoiled with homemade baked goods.

~Genevieve Kuchinsky, Nurse Practitioner

I live my purpose by helping make a difference for people every day. I believe that it is a spiritual calling and a great honor to share your gifts to help those in need. Nursing is the perfect field for living that purpose. I have been a Registered Nurse for 18 years in critical care and I've been a Nurse Practitioner for six years in critical care and family practice. I would absolutely choose nursing again. Being in this profession has been an amazing journey.

You can truly "see" who your patients are by genuinely listening to them and trying to view the world through their eyes. Respecting their personal experiences and perspectives not only promotes a trusting and caring therapeutic partnership; it also humbles your soul and positively shapes your ever-evolving practice. Interestingly, a unique experience with one patient— something that personally impressed upon you while caring for them— can indirectly help impact others' future care.

Both these quotes remind me to always stay humble and to keep an open mind and optimistic attitude about any new challenges coming my way:

"Save one person and you're a hero. Save a hundred and you're a nurse." - Anonymous

And

"The fool doth think he is wise, but the wise man knows himself to be a fool." - Shakespeare, As You Like It

Despite all of the adrenalizing life-saving events, the memories that stand out the most are the bittersweet but good deaths. Knowing that you had the compassion and strength to help provide a dignified and peaceful death while relinquishing fate to God's hands is most impacting and powerful to me.

~Holly Leahy, Nurse Practitioner

My job title is Nurse Practitioner for the Advanced Heart Failure, Mechanical Circulatory Support Device, Cardiac Transplant and Pulmonary Hypertension Team. I have been in this role for seven years— five years with Aurora and two years with Froedtert and the Medical College.

Cardiology has always been my primary love and interest. When I first heard of LVAD's (Left Ventricular Assist Devices) and Heart Transplants, I was a Nursing Assistant (fresh out of high school) and still in Nursing School. I just knew that I had to go further and do more to somehow get to work in that field one day. I wanted to be a surgeon but for personal reasons and choices, I changed my path to nursing and then a graduate degree.

I would definitely continue to do what I am doing now. However, every now and then I do think of what it would've been like to pursue my first dream of going to medical school and pursuing cardiovascular surgery.

From the clinical side of things, I have learned not to take your health or the people you love for granted. From the professional aspect, I have learned that it is okay to ask questions and admit when you don't know something. When I was a new Nurse Practitioner, I felt like I had to know all of the answers to prove myself and show my knowledge. The longer that I have practiced, the more comfortable I have become acknowledging when I don't know something. It has given me the opportunity to learn more.

There are so many answers to the question, "What motivates me?" I have always tried to be a perfectionist. Being better than the day prior and growing everyday is my main personal/professional motivator. I want to look back on my career and feel like I have made a positive impact on people's lives by supporting them or cheering them on through their battles. My daughter and stepdaughter are my other motivators. I want to show them what it is to be a strong, independent, intelligent and hard-working woman. I want to encourage them to dream big and set big goals for themselves.

My favorite quote is the Serenity Prayer:

> "God grant me the serenity to accept the
> things I cannot change;
> courage to change the things I can; and
> wisdom to know the difference."

I have applied this to my practice working in my current population almost daily. Unfortunately, there are some patients that you cannot "fix." You can only be there for them in the final stages of their disease process. The courage part helps me to make sure that I am always advocating for my patient or for the appropriate treatment strategy even when it may not be what other providers see as the correct way or when there is no consensus among the different teams involved.

What is my most memorable experience? This is another tough one to answer! Some of my happiest or most satisfying memories come from simply making the call or walking into a patient room to tell them, "We've found an organ donor" and watching their bittersweet happiness and graciousness. Seeing patients do well post heart transplant is a huge reward. My absolute favorite moment is being the first person to listen to the heartbeat of a new heart transplant recipient. It brings tears to my eyes every time.

There are other memories— less joyous but comprise a big part of my position— that still stand out. They are taking care of end stage heart failure patients and assisting them to make end of life decisions. It's helping them to be comfortable and simply being present to support them and their families as they pass away.

~Jessica Takach, APNP
Nurse Practitioner

I have only been a Nurse Practitioner for approximately one year. Prior to that I was a bedside ICU nurse for six years.

I chose nursing in order to help people in their time of need. I was drawn to critical care because I was interested in the knowledge and challenge that the role would provide. Becoming a Nurse Practitioner was another opportunity to push and challenge myself and to continue to make a difference. On harder days, I question if I chose the right job. But the moments of success or happiness make it all worth it. In the end I could not see myself doing anything else.

When I was just starting in this profession, an experienced nurse told me this about getting reported by a difficult patient: "Do not let someone else tell you how your day is going to be. Do not make judgments on your patient. Take each day as it comes and get through it with a positive attitude."

The opportunity to make a difference in the lives of others is what keeps me going. Our patients are real people with real lives outside of this hospital. They're not just a patient, a number, or a diagnosis.

Early on in my career, I remember caring for a patient who was in the ICU for an extended period of time. As caregivers, we got to know the patient and his family well. Unfortunately, the patient did not survive. His wife came back to speak to us, and thanked me personally for caring for him as a human being rather than just a patient. It was something as simple as letting him change his ostomy by himself, allowing him to feel happy about being able to do something for himself for a change. In a situation where so much certainty and control are lost, he was still able to care for himself in simple ways. I remember that moment, getting the sense that he was overwhelmed with everyone constantly doing something for him. It was that situation that helped me realize I made the right choice, that I had the intuition and compassion to be a nurse and to help people in more ways than just using my medical knowledge.

~Jesslyn McMahon, Nurse Practitioner

I chose this profession because I was sick with Pyloric Stenosis as an infant. (Pyloric stenosis is the swelling of the muscle between the stomach and the intestines, causing severe vomiting in the first few months of life.)

This disease is known to be a hereditary condition but strangely, it was not in my family genetics. It is also not common to first-born females like me. Needless to say, my parents were not prepared to handle my infantile condition. Every time my parents fed me, I would spit up. Eventually the spitting up turned into throwing up, which eventually led to projectile vomiting. My parents took me to a doctor who kept telling them I was allergic to formula. His recommended solution was to try different formula brands.

One morning, my mom came home to the smell of vomit. When she picked me up from my crib, she noticed I was turning blue and not breathing. Apparently, I had vomited and aspirated after falling asleep from feeding. She immediately scooped the vomit out of my mouth and rushed me to the emergency room. The emergency room doctors told my parents that there was nothing wrong with me and that it was unlucky that I had aspirated on my vomit. They felt I would have a minimal chance of surviving. They suggested that I be baptized immediately.

My parents refused to give up. A nurse noticed an olive-shaped mass in my stomach and she pointed it out to the doctor. The doctor offered to complete one more test by having me swallow barium. It was to determine if there was any blockage in my small intestine. That was when they found out I had pyloric stenosis. At that point I was so dehydrated and malnourished that the only IV access available was through my head. I was emergently taken to surgery to correct the problem. This experience scared my parents but helped them to be highly aware of the condition. By the time my younger brother was born with a similar problem, they were able to address it immediately.

Having this knowledge growing up, I always considered the medical field. The nurse who noticed the olive-shaped mass in my stomach saved my life. Without her, I wouldn't be here today. It was she who inspired me to consider healthcare. I also heard the stories of my cousin who is a transport nurse for a children's hospital. Those stories reminded me of my experience as an infant and made me want to help other people who are unable to help themselves. I shadowed my cousin as a transport nurse and quickly fell in love with helping the critically ill. These are the reasons why I chose to be a Registered Nurse. I want to help make a difference and hopefully be able to give back what someone gave me– LIFE! I have been a Registered Nurse for four years.

If I could go back and do it all over again, I would be a critical care doctor. When I think back about my experience, my primary care doctor could not figure out what was wrong with me. It wasn't until a nurse detected the olive-shaped mass in my stomach and notified the ER doctor who ran one last test to determine what was causing my issues. I was then put under the care of a critical care doctor. During my time as a nurse, I have grown as a person and professionally due to the experiences I have had in healthcare with patients and the multidisciplinary team. Most of my growth as a professional has come from the mentoring and education I have received from the physicians I work with daily. These people have made me become a better nurse by challenging me to learn and do more within my scope of work. I would not be where I am today without the guidance from these amazing individuals. They have motivated me to continue my education to be a nurse practitioner. But if I had to do it all over again I would be a critical care doctor.

You only get out of your experiences what you put into them. Healthcare is ever-changing. Education as a nurse is continual and ongoing. If you choose to learn from experiences to make yourself better, you will succeed. It is important to hold yourself accountable and to take ownership of your actions. By pushing yourself to learn more and develop skills, you become more valuable. It is never a good feeling to have to rely on your coworkers to constantly help you do your job.

Just because someone has a higher degree than you does not mean they are always right. Nurses are the biggest advocates for their patients. You have a voice at a time when your patient may not. Use that voice! If you don't think something is right, say something. That one thing might change their lives. Be the patient's advocate. You never know when it's going to make the most difference. A nurse's voice definitely saved my life!

I am motivated to get up and keep going every day knowing that I am helping people who are unable to help themselves. There are times throughout your career when you will put in so much hard work and effort to help save a patient, yet it could be a long road for that patient to recover. You will never really be sure what the outcome over the recovery will be. But when that patient returns to say thank you for your hard work during a difficult time in their life, that feeling is life-changing. That moment makes you realize everything was worth it and you made a difference for that patient and their family. Because of that, they have the ability to continue to live their lives. Not everything in healthcare is butterflies and rainbows, but that moment they thank you makes all the unfortunate and hard times disappear, knowing that you made a huge difference.

I don't have a personal quote, but here are three popular sayings that keep me going every day. I often remind myself of these during times of doubt or struggle.

"It is never wrong to do the right thing."
~Mark Twain
"She believed she could, so she did."
~R.S. Grey
"Never let the fear of striking out keep you from playing the game." ~Babe Ruth

~Lindsay Acheson, Registered Nurse

I am a Stroke and Endovascular Nurse Practitioner and I've been doing this job for two months now. I chose to be a nurse practitioner so that I could help people. I specifically want to motivate people to have confidence in their ability to make healthy lifestyle choices.

This profession is challenging. I learn and grown daily because of the patients and the people I work with. I am very proud to call myself a nurse. If I were to go back in time, I would still choose to be a nurse.

This profession taught me these greatest lessons: that relationships are made from listening, that judgement is unnecessary, and that I can only control my own thoughts and actions.

I love to learn, and I always want to give the patient the best care. These are what keep me motivated.

I have two quotes that I live by. The first is my philosophy on life: "Old ways won't open new doors." The second quote is my work philosophy: "A healer does not heal you. A healer is someone who holds space for you while you awaken your inner healer, so that you may heal yourself." ~Maryam Hasnaa

The most memorable times in my career are those times when I see nurses or nursing students find their confidence and voice. I love to see their growth and their individuality shine. I love to see when patients have changed to live a healthy lifestyle, it's so inspiring.

~Lisa Brandt, Nurse Practitioner

I always wanted to be a Nurse. My mom has been a critical care nurse for 40 years. I always looked up to her and still do. There are a total of four nurses in my family and the nursing profession has been a big part of my family since I was a child.

I have been a Neuro ICU Registered Nurse for five years. I chose ICU because it allows me to focus my attention and resources on only two patients at a time. Without a doubt, I would choose nursing over again, and would not want to work anywhere besides an ICU.

I really enjoy learning. There are opportunities to learn something new from every single shift. I also love to teach precept to new nurses and teach what I have learned.

It is an honor and a privilege to care for a patient and their family on what is often the worst day of their lives. I never take it for granted. I also learned that when you are very calm, even in an emergency, you can think much more clearly.

A patient's family is one of the most important parts of the health care team. Listen to the information they provide and do not hesitate to ask them questions. They know the patient better than anyone and can provide valuable information that cannot be found in a chart.

The most memorable experience in my career was working with my peers to fulfill a patient's five wishes at the end of her life. The husband of the patient did not want to stay in the room as his wife passed away. I walked him to the front door with his daughter, made sure they were safe to drive home, and came back to the patient's room. My coworker found the patient's five wishes within her advanced directives: (1) to have scripture read to her; (2) to have someone hold her hand as she passed: (3) to have Elvis Presley music playing in the background: (4) have "How Great Though Art" sang to her; and (5) to be free from pain. The patient was on a continuous medication drip to make sure she was pain-free. As I held her hand, Jason read the scripture and played Elvis from the computer in the room. Sean sang "How Great Though Art." The patient passed shortly after her wishes were met. This was truly one of the most memorable and powerful experiences I've had as a nurse.

~Patrick Schmitt, Nurse Practitioner

I work as a Nurse Practitioner within our Endovascular team. I started in October 2019 so I have been in this role for just under one year.

My desire to be part of the Neuro Endovascular team originated from the spectacular experience I gained with this team during my neurology rotation. The doctors and nurse practitioners I worked with during my clinical rotation involved me in unique patient cases that sparked my interest in the Neuro Endovascular specialty. I am very happy with my job choice and given the chance to go back, I would make the same decision.

Even though my professional career has just started, I have already learned so much. One of the greatest lessons I have learned so far is to trust myself and not question my thoughts or physical exam findings.

I am motivated by my patients and their families. Seeing the adversity they face during their hospitalization helps me realize there is no reason I cannot get up and keep going when I am in a much less critical situation compared to them. I am also motivated by knowing my patients and their families are counting on me to always give my 100%.

"Never give up because great things take time." This is a quote that inspires me.

My most memorable (and possibly meaningful) experience in my career thus far was the first consult I performed with the Neuro Endovascular team as a student. The patient had a giant cerebral aneurysm which needed to be treated. I was able to see this patient from start to finish and visualize how our team was able to help her symptoms and quality of life.

~Payton Temp, Nurse Practitioner

I chose to become a Nurse Practitioner because I enjoyed the patient population and team that I work with regularly. The different patient presentations and diagnoses keep me interested and wanting to learn more. I've been in this position for three-and-a-half years now and I would absolutely still choose this job if I were to go back in time.

You can never take anything for granted because you are not guaranteed a tomorrow. My professional life has repeatedly shown me how quickly and severely life can change.

What greatly motivates me is helping people, particularly those who are not medically inclined and do not know what is needed to live their best lives.

I do not have a personal quote, but there is a quote that helped me to get through tough days: "Was it really a bad day or was it five bad minutes that you milked all day?"

My most memorable experience comes from when I was working third shift as a RN in the hospital. A patient had hidden in his bed two forks from his meal trays. He started detoxing in the middle of the night, yelling nonstop, and was trying to stab people with the forks any time a staff member tried to calm him down or go to the side of his bed. We were unable to give him medications because we could not get close enough to him. We ended up needing to restrain him with the assistance of three RNs, two nursing assistants, and a security guard.

~*Samantha Goedde, FNP-BC*
Nurse Practitioner

I am a Registered Nurse in the Neuro ICU. I have been in this field for 5 years. I have always had an interest in the brain and taking care of people. Through nursing school I took care of a hospital level home care patient who had a significant amount of neurological issues. I think I will always be a part of Neuro care. It is a fascinating field and I absolutely love learning more about the functioning and response of the brain.

If I could go back in time I would have chosen this field a little bit sooner. I first went into nutrition science and then found my love of nursing and the Neuro field. I love what I do but if I had the opportunity, I would either continue down the field of nursing or I would have gone down the path for my DO or be a surgeon to have a bigger impact on patients' lives.

When you see a patient in the hospital, always remember that this is probably their worst day. Try to impact their lives by making them feel better. That's not necessarily a quote but it is something that I always try to keep in the back of my mind because we run into difficult patients or families. This day may be their worst day and emotions run high. In the hospital, we need to remember that.

The greatest lesson I have learned in my professional career is respecting each other and working together as a team. We have a large multidisciplinary group and we are all trying to obtain the same goals of treating and trying to give the best care to our patients. When people offer respect and have great communication, patient care runs smoothly. Our teamwork allows both the patient and the care team to have a really good experience. I think that these things are aspects that everyone knows about and cares about, but they end up getting lost as people progress through their careers. My goal would be to live out this lesson every day of my career.

My motivation is seeing the patients and colleagues around me. I get to see some amazing things happen through treatment and recovery. I also get to see my colleagues— who are some amazing people— care for a huge diverse population in some very troubling situations. There are some difficult situations, but we get to see friends and families come together with a huge amount of support for one person. Medicine is a cool thing and can really bring out the best in people. That keeps me coming back for more.

The most memorable moment in my career is one of the busiest nights I have ever experienced. We had one open bed on the unit with a patient that was decompensating and needed to be emergently intubated. We had another patient who was becoming very agitated, needed multiple nurses to help calm him down and keep him safe from himself. The patient was kicking and punching and we needed extra help from our security team. We also had a surprise admission that ran through our doors. The patient was coding in the elevator as they were coming down for a scan. They brought the patient onto our floor and entered our last room. The intensivist was already in our unit for our emergent intubation and ran over for the coding patient. All of this was occurring at about the same time. The best part about this was that every nurse was hands-on and trying to help in any way they could. There was great communication between nurses, respiratory therapists, and doctors as we maneuvered through these frantic moments at the very early hours of the morning. No matter what happens throughout my career I look back at that night and think, "That was a terrible night." But it was also one of the most memorable moments for it demonstrated the best teamwork I have ever seen.

~Scott Simandl, Nurse Practitioner

My favorite quote is: "A mind set in its ways is wasted." – Eric Schmidt

I have been a Primary Care Nurse Practitioner for almost two years. I wanted to pursue further education beyond a Bachelor's degree as I have always enjoyed academia. I consider myself a lifelong learner, yet felt stagnant in my role as a registered nurse. I felt called to a more autonomous role wherein I could improve healthcare access and delivery.

In my short time as a nurse practitioner I've realized the importance of having a passion for your profession and letting that be your guiding force. I have also learned to embrace a growth mindset, to be patient, proactive, and curious.

I am motivated by the opportunity to impact the health of an individual, reduce suffering and to restore one's quality of life. I am motivated by complex patient presentations and the opportunity to exercise creative thinking. I am also motivated by patient satisfaction and positive feedback.

~Taylor Villwock, Nurse Practitioner

CHAPTER 19

Nurses

I truly like helping people. I like being the person to lean on when someone is in need. That's why I chose to be a Registered Nurse. I've been in this role for more than four years and I would choose this job again if I were to go back in time. Knowing I am making a difference motivates me on this job.

Three things I've learned in this profession:

> (1) Take everything as a learning experience.
> (2) Don't do drugs.
> (3) A headache may be more than just a headache.

What comprises my most memorable experiences are those instances when I catch neuro changes. There is no better feeling than having my knowledge, experience, and instinct help a patient.

~Abigail Anger, Registered Nurse

—————>>●<<—————

I've been a Registered Nurse in the Neurosurgical ICU for more than five years. This is my first job out of nursing school. I was recruited by the manager at the time (Linda) when I had no experience in an ICU before. I was open to all opportunities but really loved the camaraderie of the team on the unit. I fell in love with the job from there!

I would definitely still be where I am today. As a nurse in the hospital you get sent to float to other units from time to time. I've had the opportunity to experience a variety of patient populations. But I've found my niche in my neurosurgical patient population. I love the physicians I get to work with on a daily basis, the staff, and the management. I would say that my experience in the Neuro ICU, while definitely stressful at times, has been an overall positive one. We're a team and a family here.

I have learned so many great lessons from this profession: Rely on your teammates and be there for one another. We are all a team. As a team, it is our responsibility to help our patients. Our goal should be one and the same. Being in the ICU is a stressful and fast-paced environment and it's important that we are there for our patients every minute. When your patient is in a critical situation, don't be afraid to ask for help. It benefits the patient in the end. Always collaborate with your team members to ensure the best outcome for your patient.

Knowing that not every patient will make it is a hard reality to come to terms with, but our team is excellent at what we do and we are sometimes able to turn desperate situations into successful outcomes. What keeps me going are those successes and recognizing that we are giving patients every opportunity to do well.

"Just keep swimming!" That is a great quote. It truly does apply to all situations in the ICU. Keep your head above water and use what you have to keep going. Lean on your friends, family, and coworkers, and you can keep yourself and your patients afloat.

One of my most memorable experiences is when I had a very critical younger patient whose family had to fly in from another country. The parents were mainly Spanish-speaking. I spoke Spanish most of my life, so I would engage with them by speaking in Spanish. I wanted to help them feel more comfortable with the situation. On one particular occasion, when I was not directly taking care of their son, the father came over to me and started speaking to me in Spanish. His reasoning? He wanted to give me an opportunity to practice. His son was in critical condition and yet he chose to come over and practice Spanish with me. It made me realize that he had come to trust me. It truly touched me that I had made an impact on him.

~Alexandra Stone, Registered Nurse

———➤◆◆◆———

Looking back, deciding to become a nurse was one of the easiest decisions of my life. I am the oldest of five kids, three of whom are on the autism spectrum and have various other medical problems. Because of this, I encountered so many nurses and doctors during my childhood. I noticed what an impact some of these individuals had on my family and the overall outcome of my siblings' care. To me, being in the medical field and welding knowledge and compassion together would be the greatest honor. From the example of my parents, I learned the importance of implementing acceptance of all people, regardless of ability and compassion, into my everyday life. I knew I would want to emphasize this in my career, so becoming a nurse was naturally the perfect fit.

I am still learning so much since I have only been a Registered Nurse for a year. As my coworkers say, nursing is a career of lifelong learning. One of the greatest lessons I can recall is the importance of communication and advocacy amongst healthcare providers for patients. Communication is crucial amongst those caring for the patient as well as between healthcare providers and the patient and their family. Effective communication helps to ensure the safety of the patient while involving them in their own care. In my role as a nurse, taking the time to explain and communicate aspects of care can decrease patient anxiety and can promote compliance with the plan of care during the hospital stay and at discharge.

Nursing is hard. It embodies a much greater role of coordination, communication, and advocacy than I had originally realized. However difficult it may be on a daily basis, I have never doubted my decision to become a nurse. I feel so lucky to go into work every day with a new challenge and a new opportunity to optimize the care my patients are receiving.

What drives me is my desire to learn and my love for working with people. I love the challenge and new experiences that each day brings with my career. I love being able to think critically and being innovative with my care. One of my goals for the next few years is to go back to school so that I can teach Nursing. I also would like to take some Spanish courses so that I can communicate more effectively with some of our patient population. My nursing career motivates me to continue learning and be open to new experiences and change.

One of my favorite quotes is by Fr. Pedro Arrupe, a Jesuit priest dedicated to serving the poor and the marginalized. I heard this first in high school and it has followed me ever since: "Fall in love, stay in love, and it will decide everything." I know that this quote is used in many wedding ceremonies, but I took it to heart as it concerns my career as a nurse. I fell in love with Nursing on my first day of class at Marquette University. Despite certain hardships and difficulty throughout my transition from school to career, I prioritize reflection on the positive aspects of my job. I can always think of a more impactful and moving experience as a nurse that puts any difficult situations into perspective. This is how I "stay in love" with my career and stay motivated to working towards bettering myself as a nurse and an individual.

My most memorable experience involves a patient who was hospitalized on my unit for a few weeks. He was very sick and weak. I had the privilege of being his nurse every time I worked for continuity of care. He had a lot of support from family and friends, so someone he loved was always with him. Hence, I became very close with him and his family during this difficult time. It was during his stay that I realized how my role can truly impact a patient and their family. I communicated with them effectively, reiterating what doctors and other healthcare providers had said or written in the chart regarding the plan of care. I made an effort to make the patient comfortable and encouraged him to move around the room with me to build up his strength. When he started to deteriorate, I listened to the doctor discuss goals of care and offer realistic options. As difficult as this was, I noted how the family's mindset had shifted with this effective communication style. Instead of exhausting further medical efforts that would have rendered ineffective or initiated false hope, the family was able to focus on making him comfortable and spending quality time with him during his final days. I was able to participate as well, talking with them about memories and the patient's favorite things. When he passed, it was peaceful. There were no surprises. I will never forget how kind and honest the doctor was, and how his effective communication brought peace to the patient and his family.

~*Alexandra Wiskes, Registered Nurse*

"The best way to find yourself is to lose yourself in the service of others" - Mahatma Gandhi (the original quote)

Knowing that I am making a difference in someone's life motivates me. I take pride in being able to help and care for a patient when they are at their sickest.

I always had a passion for the medical field. Early on, I knew I wanted to work in healthcare. I initially went for medical assisting and then worked my way towards becoming a Registered Nurse. I specifically chose Neuro ICU because I have a family history of neurological conditions such as multiple sclerosis and ischemic strokes. I also had a close family friend pass away from a ruptured AVM (arteriovenous malformation). That being said, Neuro holds a spot in my heart because I know how much this patient population endures and I want to help in any way that I can.

If I could go back in time I would have gone to medical school right out of high school. I worked in orthopedics for several years, and orthopedic surgery always was of interest to me.

This profession taught me to trust that every day is going to be a great day and to always learn from it. As a new nurse, there are many things that I simply do not know. Sometimes it can make you feel defeated, but that is normal. Expanding your knowledge and skill set is continuous. Medical professionals are learning and improving each day, and I think that is the beauty of healthcare.

Being a fairly new nurse (I've only been in this position for three months), my most memorable experience has been hearing about the outcome of a patient. He was young and had a tumor on his brainstem that he had surgically dissected. He had a poor prognosis, was intubated and sedated. But during his hospital stay, he significantly improved and was eventually discharged. The patient came back to thank the staff for all of their help. He stated that even though he was intubated/sedated during his hospitalization, he still remembers conversations we've had with him as well as the music/movies that were played. He had a pretty incredible recovery. It's also remarkable that even if patients do not appear to be conscious, they are still very much present.

~ Alicia Mueller, Registered Nurse

My dad had cancer when I was a child, so I spent a lot of time in hospitals while growing up. The nurses who took care of him were so kind and compassionate. They provided great care for my dad and helped make the hospital less scary for me during a time that was filled with unknowns. The nurses did everything from making gloves into balloon turkeys for me on Thanksgiving, to sitting and talking with me, and explaining what they were doing while caring for my dad. In high school, I attended a health care careers camp which provided me the opportunity to shadow a nurse on a medical surgical floor which reinforced my passion for nursing. I am now a Registered Nurse working on an Inpatient Neurology Unit and I've been an RN for about four years. I have learned to always keep learning and not be scared to ask questions in this profession.

Nursing has taught me so much about myself and what I value. It has provided me the opportunity to appreciate people from all different backgrounds and life experiences. Every day I get the opportunity to care for people during times of uncertainty and help allay their fears by providing compassionate care when they are most vulnerable. I also appreciate how nursing allows me to use my critical thinking skills while collaborating with other members of the healthcare team (MD's, therapists, pharmacists, etc.). Although it can be stressful at times, I can't imagine doing anything else.

> "Vulnerability is the center of shame,
> scarcity, fear, anxiety, and uncertainty, but
> it is also the birthplace of love, belonging,
> and joy." ~Brene Brown

I find this quote inspiring because as a nurse I am constantly asking people to be vulnerable with me so I can help them. Providing a space where people feel safe enough to be vulnerable is always my goal because that is how I am able to be most helpful. Knowing that I can make someone's day better— by helping them feel heard and advocating for them in their time of vulnerability— is what motivates me each day. You never know someone else's burdens, so being able to add a little light into someone's life is always something that brings me joy.

I was caring for a patient who had significant difficulties speaking due to a stroke. I was lucky enough to care for her early in her hospitalization through her discharge. During that time, I was able to get to know her and learn about her life experiences— both her times of joy, like when she met her daughter, and her times of struggles, like when she escaped an abusive marriage. More than a year later, the patient was readmitted. As soon as I saw her name, I remembered her. I walked into her room to introduce myself as her nurse for the day. With a big grin on her face, she pointed right at me and said, "You! You! You! Come over here!" Her difficulty communicating remained, but I knew she instantly remembered me. I felt honored that I had left such a positive impact on her and that she had remembered me even over a year later.

~Anonymous 1, Registered Nurse

I am a Registered Nurse. I'm proud to be a nurse and that I'm able to help others. Nursing has been my profession for 20 years. Since I was little, I wanted to be a nurse. Being a nurse kind of ran in my family, you could say. Two out of three siblings are in the healthcare field and starting off as a bedside nurse. If I were to turn back time, I would still be a nurse but I'd probably go to school to become a Nurse Practitioner.

The greatest lesson I've learned as a nurse is that every day is a gift from God. No one knows when his/her last day will be, so live your life to be a good person and to be happy.

What makes my job special and memorable? I guess it's just the simple things that seem to make a difference with patients' families. When they write a thank you note mentioning you by name and sharing how much you helped get them through a rough time, that makes me proud of my job.

One of my favorite quotes is by Helen Keller: "The most beautiful things in the world cannot be seen or even touched. They must be felt with the heart."

~Anonymous 2, Registered Nurse

I am a Nursing Professional Development Generalist (Nurse Educator). This is a new role for the hospital and I've held this position for six months. Prior to this, I have been a nurse at Aurora St. Luke's Medical Center (ASLMC) for nine years in various positions, keeping Neuro and Neurosurgery as my specialty.

When I was a new graduate from nursing school, I was desperate for any job. I ended up landing a job in the Neuro ICU right out of school and fell in love with it. I have a deep passion for helping people and doing all I can to help remove barriers or assist them when they are going through hard times.

I discovered early in my Neuro career how patients and families heavily relied on us as healthcare professionals to help them navigate through life-altering medical diagnoses. I was selfish for a time and wanted to see where my RN degree could take me. I took a position in the outpatient Neurosurgery clinic where I deepened my passion for helping people and sharing the knowledge that I had gained working in Neuro ICU. In the Aurora Neuroscience Innovation Institute (ANII) clinic, my passion for helping others expanded not only to patients but also to my fellow team members. I loved sharing with them the knowledge and experiences I gained over the years.

I moved back to the hospital setting where I had a broad focus on clinical education and professional development of our ICU nurses. As the organization changed, so did my position. I transitioned into a Nursing and Professional Development Generalist for Neuro ICU & Inpatient Rehab unit in the winter of 2019.

In my new role, I find great pride in sharing my professional and personal experiences with ASLMC. It brings me great joy to see people achieve their goals. All the roles I have assumed at ASLMC have somehow presented themselves. I feel that I must give back to the organization that helps me find a purpose in life and to fulfill what I was set out to do. I would never want to change what I have experienced. I have learned many life lessons from all of my roles. I will identify as a nurse all my life.

I have been a patient in Neuro ICU myself. To be on the other side and relying on others was eye-opening and memorable. I had a small posterior fossa meningioma removed in early May of 2019. The surgery went well. However, I was having headaches and not healing properly. I needed to have a lumbar drain and second surgery in mid-June of 2019 requiring an 18-day stay in the hospital.

There are people out there every day that need help. One day in the healthcare profession is never the same and always presents new challenges. We can only get better each day!

Life is short and we must live it to the fullest every day. We never know what could happen to us so we must enjoy every moment of it! When life presents challenges, we must take it one day at a time and make the best of out the cards we are dealt. Seeing patients come in with a life altering stroke or a new diagnosis of a brain tumor is something that can happen quickly and change your life so greatly.

This quote was shared with me early in the COVID pandemic and it resonates with me daily: "Leadership is about making others better as a result of your presence and making sure that impact lasts in your absence." ~Sheryl Sandberg, COO Facebook

Here's another quote that I love and is my philosophy, "When you believe in someone, you profoundly increase their ability to have faith in themselves. When you love someone, you imprint on their heart something so powerful that it changes the trajectory of their life. When you do both, you set into motion a gift to the world… because those who are believed in and loved understand the beauty of a legacy and the absolute duty of paying it forward." ~Jason Varsey, A Walk with Prudence

~Anonymous 3, Registered Nurse

⇒⭢●⭠⇐

"Be the change that you wish to see in the world." I live by this quote by Mahatma Gandhi.

The ability to help others is one of the reasons I chose to be a nurse. I've been Registered Nurse Coordinator for less than a year. Before my current position, I was in Neuro ICU for three years. Positive success stories are what keep me going in this job. But I know that no matter how hard we try, we cannot heal every patient.

My most memorable experience was when I was working in Neuro ICU and admitted a stroke patient who went immediately to interventional radiology. She could not talk at all or follow any commands. When the clot was taken out, the patient was immediately better and was able to talk within seconds. It was an amazing thing to see!

~Anonymous 4, Registered Nurse

———◄●►———

I was inspired to become a nurse and help the sick when my grandfather was very ill. I've been a Registered Nurse for almost eight years. I would still choose this job if I were to travel back in time. I like the flexibility and the many options it offers, but I would have gone to a tech school versus a university. My college debt is a heavy weight on my shoulders.

What motivates me? With this job, I am able to support my family. By carrying on with my job, I am able to teach my daughter independence. I also like my co-workers and they help to keep me going.

In my professional life, I learned that you should enjoy what you do, and that you should keep challenging yourself. I always say "I'm living the dream," and I am. I have a home, a car, a job, a beautiful family. I am healthy and I can walk.

I have many memorable experiences throughout my career. Most recently, I was able to restore confidence in my patients and help them manage their fears. I do this by holding their hands and using my knowledge to teach them how to cope.

~Anonymous 5, Registered Nurse

———⟫◈⟪———

I have been working as a Registered Nurse/Nursing Supervisor for eight months. I was ready to take the next step in my nursing career by going into leadership. My current role provides the perfect opportunity to utilize my nursing skills while leading a nursing team. I would still choose this job if I went back in time. I love working in healthcare and could not see myself working in another field.

One of greatest lessons I have learned in my professional life is to not take things personally. It can be easy to let others' comments and criticisms weigh you down, but you should be able to listen and grow from the comments and not let them get to you.

My drive to live a successful life for myself, my husband, and our future family motivates me to keep going. I want to provide a life for my family that can lessen stress and burden.

Growing up, my parents always instilled in my siblings and me to treat people the way you would want to be treated. I constantly use this phrase to lead me in my practice when caring for vulnerable patient populations.

It's hard to choose one of the most memorable experiences in my career because I have experienced so many memorable moments that have shaped me into the nurse I am today. I feel that any time I have cared for a patient during end-of-life, I have learned something new about myself as a person and have developed a new outlook on life.

~Anonymous 6, Registered Nurse

———————

I have been with Aurora Neurosciences Innovation Institute (ANII) for more than five years. Over the course of that period, I went back to school for my Registered

Nurse license and I naturally climbed the ladder to be in the position I am in now.

I am currently a Care Coordinator and I have only been in this role for three months. Previously, I was a clinic Registered Nurse and ENT for five months. I was also a Licensed Practical Nurse (LPN)/Scribe for more than four years.

Getting my RN license is my most memorable experience! When I started with Aurora, I was content in my position. But being around so many intelligent and innovative people, I was inspired to go back to school, get my RN license, and continue to grow. Working here has granted me so many opportunities.

Nothing is easy. I have learned to balance work, school, and family life. Finding ME time is hard but I do my best to make sure I get some.

My family is my biggest motivator. I want to be better for myself so I can be better for them.

~Anonymous 7, Registered Nurse

My job title is Registered Nurse. I have been working in healthcare services for 30 years providing assistance and support for the critically ill and for any other needs of the community. I began my healthcare journey as a Physical Therapist Assistant. I felt that I could offer more in the acute care setting, so I pushed myself to earn my Emergency Medical Technician License and provide care in the ER. I became so interested in emergency medicine that I went to nursing school to be able to give even more care to the populations that I serve.

I have encountered some of the most precious people and families that have faced, and risen above, some of life's most challenging situations. Spouses and families have to process and decide life and death decisions in a heartbeat. That is true courage.

I have learned that if I offer kindness and respect first, most of the time I will be on the receiving end of a softer and calmer person.

I especially enjoy the quote from the Dalai Lama: "Our main purpose on earth is to help each other and if we can't do that, at least don't hurt each other." I am motivated by collaborating with my co-workers, the ER physicians, the patients and their families to meet varying healthcare needs within a complex community. I love the challenge of finding creative ways to return people to their homes in the safest manner possible.

There was a 75-year-old female patient who had lost and regained her pulse many times during a cardiac arrest. It happened a few days before Christmas. Her son came into the ER and loudly encouraged her, "Come on, Mom! You have been through worse than this!" Finally, the woman regained both pulse and blood pressure and was later transferred to the ICU. That is one of my most memorable moments in my career.

~Anonymous 8, Registered Nurse

My grandmother suggested that I take up Nursing. She was a Registered Nurse who graduated in the 1930s. She said, "It is a good job, and always something to fall back on if you decide to try something else." On good days at work, I send a thank you to my grandma. On bad days, I ask her what she was thinking. So far, she has not answered.

I have been a Registered Nurse for 23 years; the last 11 in Radiology. Personally, I learned not to tell people I'm a nurse. They always want to tell me their medical problems or ask advice.

Professionally, I try to learn from every experience. There might be better ways of doing something, or better ways of interacting with patients, families, or co-workers. It is an awesome feeling when you've made a difference in the lives of others, whether with small comforting acts or big life-saving things.

I always try to remember the Golden Rule I learned as a kid: "Do unto others as you would want them to do unto you." I always try to treat patients like I would want my family treated.

~Auntie Goose, Registered Nurse

[Note: In the section about the author at the end of this book, the origin of Team Goose is explained. This beloved nurse, who is a great aunt to her nieces, has rightfully earned the title of Auntie Goose.]

I am a Vascular Access Registered Nurse. I have been a nurse for 15 years and this job is something I always wanted to do.

When I was working as a staff nurse on a med/surg step down unit, I felt stuck and frustrated with Nursing. I felt more like a slave and a servant rather than being there to help people get well and stay well. Since I left bedside nursing and transitioned into specialty fields, I feel needed, appreciated, and valued as a caregiver and employee.

I work with great people and I get awesome support. I found that who you work with, and who you work for, both play a big part in your perception of value, appreciation, and acceptance in your work life.

Also, you should never stop trying to achieve the greatness you want in your life. It may take a while but if you don't give up and keep striving for what you want, you will eventually get it (greatness & happiness).

"Believe you can achieve." I don't remember where this quote is from. Lol! I just always follow the guidance of believing in yourself. No one else can believe in you more than yourself. Otherwise, it's not gonna happen.

My most memorable experience was holding a dying patient's hand while he took his last breath.

~Benita Cruz, Registered Nurse

————✄————

I'm an Emergency Department Flow Coordinator RN. I have been in this role for three years, but I've have been an Emergency Department Nurse for six years now at St. Luke's.

It has been an extremely rewarding and eye-opening career so far. I see people on some of the worst and best days of their lives, and I've seen how we, as healthcare workers, are able to make such a positive impact with these individuals. There are times when we are literally saving a life. There is no greater accomplishment or feeling from seeing them stabilize and walk out of the hospital with a great outlook ahead of them.

Every day is different in the ED (Emergency Department) and I can honestly say that no day at work is ever boring. After staffing bedside for a while, I also became interested in Flow and helping the department function more efficiently. This is when I took the ED Flow Coordinator position that was newly created a couple of years ago. I get to be a part of the leadership team while still having work relationships with the ED nurses. This position allows me to help drive and meet metrics, resolve barriers and delays, and make sure patients get where they need to go in a timely manner. It gives me such satisfaction to have an empty waiting room!

Initially, I went to college to be an MD. In one semester, I even switched to being a Dentist. Now that I have been in Nursing for nearly seven years, I would not change my career choice. The reward of the job is worth it. There are days, though, that I still contemplate leaving Nursing completely and opening a bakery.

What is the greatest lesson that I've learned in my professional life? Do not take life for granted, period. Life is too short. So, eat that cake and jump out of that plane!

I am highly motivated to keep going by my 10-year-old daughter and knowing that I am in a career that makes a positive impact on others. I am guided by Maya Angelou's quote "Try to be a rainbow in someone's cloud."

Here's one of my most memorable experiences in my career:

We had an elderly patient who was found down in her hoarder home. She was unconscious for an unknown amount of time. It was winter. A pipe leaked and the patient was found lying in freezing water in her home. She was brought in as a PNB (Pulseless Non-Breather). We warmed her and cared for her for hours in the ED with every intervention possible. Patient went to ICU with the LUCAS machine (a mechanical chest compression device used for life-saving purposes) still running. Her outlook seemed poor from labs/imaging results. Thankfully, the patient was revived and was later discharged. A month later, we saw her back in the ED, complaining of leg pain. We also assisted her in finding safe housing. It was so incredible to see her back to decent health after such an ordeal. It was amazing!!! Thank God for the frozen water on the floor, it preserved her heart and brain. It saved her life!

~Caitlin McLaughlin, BSN, Registered Nurse

There are too many memorable experiences to count like all of my firsts in nursing— first code, death, 'save', error, and doctor calls. Other memorable moments include training fellow nurses all of what I have learned; and leading teams of nursing/caregivers to deliver the best care possible. It's easy to get wrapped up in healthcare politics. But I keep patient safety in the forefront of my mind. My best memories are all the patients I have helped over the years by simply caring for them and doing my job.

I am currently a Nurse Coordinator. I have been doing this particular job for more than three years. I have been a Registered Nurse for 12 years. I chose nursing because as cliché as it sounds, I like to help people. I am also intrigued by healthcare in general. I would absolutely choose this career again. I have learned so much and have had great opportunities to help patients and fellow caregivers over the years.

The greatest lesson I have learned is you don't know what you don't know. The best thing you can do is ASK and speak up!

My patients make me get up and keep going. Each and every one of them hold a special story in life. They are all different and have had an exciting journey in regards to their health and how they got to me.

"Take ONE day at a time." I'm not sure where this quote originated but it really sticks with me. Thinking too far in the future especially with something acutely going on can make one more anxious and stressed out. Always think about the patient.

~Cassandra, BSN, Registered Nurse

I'll be a Registered Nurse (RN) for almost five years in March. I have been in the medical field for about 10 years as a Certified Nursing Assistant (CNA) and Licensed Vocational Nurse (LVN) prior to becoming an RN.

As a little girl I always wanted to be a doctor and always played the role of a doctor. I ended up going to school for cosmetology but I needed to do more especially when my single mother fell ill. I had to take over and care for the both of us. I took on a student assistant job for the state of California at Lanterman Developmental Center where I worked one-on-one with those with special needs. Later, I joined another company working one-on-one with autistic children. It was then that I realized I wanted to go back to pursuing my dream of being in the medical field. I worked multiple jobs and went to school to become an LVN. In the process I challenged the boards to become a CNA. Eventually I finished LVN school, started working home health while also being a manager at McDonald's. I was eventually offered a job as a CNA in an acute care facility, then transitioned into an LVN, and now into an RN position all at the same place. If I could back in time, I would still be a nurse. The only thing I would change is following my dream and getting it done sooner.

I have learned to face many fears. When I first became a Registered Nurse, I was fearful of making mistakes. I was fearful of patients dying. I cried during the first six months of my career because of this. But soon after, I learned that some patients would die and their families will cry. But I also learned that some patients will survive and their families will be very grateful. I learned how to provide compassionate care, how to listen, how to smile, and how much I mean to others by doing what I do.

I have always been an incredibly determined person. I set goals and do everything in my power to achieve those goals. What drives me is the desire to be successful in life. When I become a parent, I would want my children to follow my path. I want to be able to provide for my children, put them through school, and to the best of my ability, lead them to live a good life.

One of my patients once told me, "Save money but enjoy life. When you die, your money is nothing. Enjoy it now while you can." This really stuck with me because I was never able to enjoy my money. I had to become responsible at a very young age. Now I see that yes, we need to save for an emergency but there is so much to life to see and enjoy.

My most memorable experience is seeing myself grow, working my way up the ladder from CNA, to LVN, to RN. It is always a great feeling when other seasoned nurses compliment me. They have watched me through the process and they tell others, "This girl right here is strong. She has accomplished so much."

~Darleen Hernandez, Registered Nurse

I am a Registered Nurse practicing in the specialty of Cardiology for 32 years. I have been in the role of manager for an ambulatory procedural area for six years. As a little girl I always knew that I wanted to be a nurse. I think that the need to care for people was ingrained into my DNA. If I could go back in time, I would only change some of the small decisions I made regarding jobs status. I love being a nurse and spending time with people in order to help them in any way possible.

I have learned that had I not had a waitress job in college I would not have been prepared for my nursing career. That first job experience taught me how important it is to have good customer service skills. It is so important that the customer is the focus of the service delivered or the care given.

"Treat each individual as if you were treating your own mother or father." This quote inspires me. My commitment to patients and my team each day gets me going. They are the reason I get up and go energetically each day.

When I was a younger and new as a nurse, I worked with post heart bypass patients on a step-down heart surgical unit. We cared for patients from all over the world and it was an amazing adventure. I had a patient from Israel and he had very strict religious routines with prayer each morning. I recall walking into his room 24 hours post-surgery to find him praying while kneeling on the floor with his chest tubes stretched tight. Needless to say, I was a bit taken by surprise. I made sure he was ok and stayed by his side while he prayed. When he was finished, he held my hand and thanked me for the care and commitment I offered him. He said to me, "Thank you for praying with me!" I will never forget this experience and how one small moment can mean so much to an individual.

~Dawn Vajgrt, Registered Nurse

My job title currently is Travel Registered Nurse. I have been a Travel RN since 2007. I have been an RN since 1981. I have done many kinds of nursing. I actually retired from the state of Florida in 2005 after 20 years. My last title with the State of Florida was Registered Nurse Consultant.

I don't know if I chose nursing or if it chose me. I wanted to be a nurse since second grade. Either my twin or I won a trip to a girl scout summer camp. My parents paid for the other so we could both go (which I'm sure was hard for them because we were not rich). I hated being in summer camp. Almost every day I would pretend I was sick, and I'd be sent to the nurse's office. I loved it in there. To this day I still remember the counter top with Q tips, tongue blades, etc. From that summer forward, I knew I wanted to be a nurse.

I've never regretted being in this career and I'd definitely choose it again. One of my sisters is a multi-millionaire from working in the corporate world. I truly believe I am richer than her because of my meaningful work. I make a difference in people's lives.

The greatest lesson I learned in my professional life is that no matter who you are, how rich or famous you are, you're still a human being whose body functions the same as everyone else's. No one is getting out of this life alive. We need to appreciate every day we have on this earth because tomorrow is not promised to us.

Right now, I'm working in Interventional Radiology. My patients motivate me to get up and keep going. I know I make a difference in my patients' lives, even if it's only for a couple of hours. I know whether I'm getting them ready for a procedure, helping them during the procedure, or recovering them from a procedure, I'm going to make their experience the best I can. And hopefully they will remember the excellent care and compassion I gave them. Many times, patients come back for multiple procedures in Interventional Radiology. I want them to have a positive experience the first time so they won't be anxious and afraid when they come back.

I worked in Nursing Administration for many years. I had a wonderful mentor. Early in my career she told me "Dorothy, you don't have to win every battle, as long as you win the war." That quote came in very handy during my career in Administration. Another quote I love that I tell my patients frequently is: "Tough times don't last, but tough people do." Robert Schuller, a preacher, wrote a book with that title. If you can get past the part about his tough time building a 3-million-dollar cathedral, it really has some good advice in it. Another one I remember is: "Don't cut down the tree in wintertime" or something to that effect. In other words, don't rush to make decisions. Of course, the tree will be bare in winter. Wait 'til spring to see if it comes back to life before making any important decisions.

I honestly can't think of a most memorable experience. I've held too many hands and saved more lives than I can count. But I can honestly say I've received so much more from my patients and families than I've given them. Each person is so unique and wonderful in their own way. Almost everyone has made me appreciate life so much more.

~Dorothy Grezik, Registered Nurse

I have been working as a Registered Nurse for four years. I chose to become a nurse because I wanted to travel the country and the world working to improve the health of communities globally. My ultimate dream is to join Doctors Without Borders. In the meantime, I chose to be an ICU nurse to become among those at the bedside taking care of extremely critical patients and helping their family members through the most difficult time. Nurses get to make a huge impact on people's lives.

If I could go back in time, I would still choose this job. I started in the Neuro ICU and that is a great background to have. I recently began travel nursing so I am glad I chose this career path. I am able to travel and have a lot of flexibility with my schedule. I also don't think I would be able to sit at a desk all day, so I like that this job allows me to move around and be on my feet. At times, this job can be stressful and trying but for the most part, it is really rewarding.

What motivates me to get up and keep going is the fact that I want to be better every day. The greatest lessons I have learned in my professional life are: (1) to always keep a professional attitude; and (2) to stand up for yourself when conflict arises. I also think it's important to keep a level head in stressful situations.

Here are a few quotes that have helped me and inspired me:

> "Be who you are and say what you feel
> because those who mind don't matter and
> those who matter don't mind." ~Dr. Seuss

"Get busy living or get busy dying."
~Shawshank Redemption

"Twenty years from now you will be more
disappointed by the things you didn't do
than by the ones you did do. So throw
off the bowlines. Sail away from the safe
harbor. Catch the trade winds in your sails.
Explore. Dream. Discover." ~Mark Twain

During one busy night shift, I took care of a woman who crashed during the day. She was extremely sick and in critical condition. Her brain bleed increased and they started her on CVVH (Continuous Veno-Venous Hemofiltration). I was so extremely busy all night and barely had a chance to sit down. At the end of my shift, her blood pressure tanked to the 60s/30s. The Nurse Practitioner and doctor were at the bedside. They brought the family in and decided to let her go. It was extremely discouraging because I felt like I worked so hard and did my best to save her/take care of her and my efforts were futile. The family was very upset and the husband started crying in the room at the end of the shift and it was heartbreaking.

~*Ekaterin Kovatch, Registered Nurse*

For almost nine years I've worked as a Registered Nurse in the Neuro ICU. I had an extern position in this unit and the manager was amazing. I did not want to start my nursing career in a specialized ICU, but I wouldn't change a thing if I could go back in time.

I've learned that in this profession, collaboration is key.

My mother and grandmother taught me to be kind and helpful. I live by this. I believe that I am doing God's work by taking care of patients when they need it most. I learn something new every day at work. Every day.

I once took care of a pregnant momma who found out she had a brain tumor. Ultimately, she lost her baby and almost two years later, she lost her battle. She was my most memorable patient.

~ Elizabeth Dellemann, Registered Nurse

I actually wanted to be a microbiologist when I was younger. However, I started working in retail when I was in high school and I enjoyed working with people. I really loved science so in my senior year of high school I took a Certified Nursing Assistant course. It was the hardest course I ever took because the hands-on portion of the class was so different from all my other courses. It turned out to be the best course I ever took. It challenged me in terms of physiological and interactive scientific thinking as an introduction to Nursing. After that, I never looked back. I wanted to be a nurse.

For a little over four months now, I've been a Registered Nurse in the Neuro ICU at St. Luke's Medical Center in Milwaukee. I have been a nurse for more than three years. My background includes Medical-Surgical/Neurology.

I always thought: if I ever won the lottery, would I still be a nurse? Yes! I enjoy my job in terms of the people I work with and the people I meet. There are many people of different backgrounds in both Milwaukee and the suburbs of Chicago where I used to work. I also volunteer on international medical trips and I've had the opportunity to travel to Haiti and El Salvador on one of those medical missions. I still haven't found another job that allows me to take care of people at their most vulnerable times of their lives or a job that offers so many opportunities to help others as an RN.

I think the greatest lesson I have learned as a nurse has nothing to do with my professional skills, but rather my attitude— towards my patients, our healthcare system, and our society as a whole. When you travel to countries, such as Haiti, that have little to no healthcare or to countries where most people have never seen a doctor in their lifetime, you gain a different perspective on what it means to be a nurse. It really makes me thankful for the healthcare we have here in this country, where we can go to any emergency room and help is provided regardless of race, ethnicity, financial status, etc. I don't expect my patients to understand, but I've learned that most people just want someone to listen to them. They don't want a solution, but just someone there who would be by their side.

Not only do my patients motivate me to keep going, but also my long term goals. As a student that continues to learn, I've always set goals for myself. I have achieved one of my goals to become an Intensive Care Nurse. Now I am working on becoming a Certified Nurse in Cardiac-Vascular, Stroke, and in a year Critical Care Nursing. I still aim to one day go back to school to become a Practitioner. I am interested in researching and conducting a dissertation to earn my Doctorate of Nurse Practitioner. I enjoy school and evidenced-based practice. Since Neurology is what I am most familiar with, I would love to work alongside a physician in the Intensive Care Unit or Neurosurgery. But I am open to whatever comes my way.

My favorite quote is: "Be fearless in the pursuit of what sets your soul on fire" ~Jennifer Lee

I've come across many obstacles in my professional career and this quote helps me to take failure as a stepping stone to reach my goals, not a step back from my journey.

One nurse told me, "If you are scared enough of something, it just means you have to learn more about it." I don't remember which nurse it was, but what she said makes me want to learn more about my patients and their conditions. I've learned to step up to the plate and learn from things that scare me, not run from them.

My most memorable experience as a nurse has been working in the Neuro ICU at St. Luke's. I've learned so much from my colleagues and co-workers and I continue to learn everyday. My preceptor, Jon Brockman, was a helpful and exceptional person who really wanted to show me why my patient was doing something and what interventions I need to take. I know Jon is passionate about his practice and I hope to one day be a valuable asset to not only this unit, but this organization.

~Emily Olszak, Registered Nurse

⟫◆⟪

I am a Registered Nurse and I have been practicing as a nurse for the past six years. I worked as a Psychiatric Nurse working with the pediatric population at Rogers Memorial Hospital for a year. Then, I decided to take my career down a different path working in the emergency department here at St. Luke's. I've been in this position for the past five years. I just recently graduated in May with Master of Science in Nursing as a Family Nurse Practitioner, and just passed my board exams! I am excited for the next step of my journey in healthcare.

My dream job was to become a Family Nurse Practitioner. I decided to embark down the journey of emergency medicine as I knew that this would give me the best, well-rounded experience in seeing a lot of different patient scenarios. I also chose this job to honor my mother who always pushed me to be my best. She could tell that I always loved to help people and take care of others, even though I would be stubborn and say, "I want to be an astronaut." My mother was in nursing school but was unable to complete her program because her father became terminally ill. It was too much for her at the time, and then she raised me and my sister. I know that I make her and my father proud because I have made it so far in my career as a nurse.

I love this career. There is so much flexibility and you can literally be any type of nurse you want! I also love the science behind the human body. I find it fascinating and there is always something more to learn as new discoveries and innovations for treatments are made. I am grateful that I chose this path because it is so versatile that you can be whatever you want to be or journey down a path that interests you.

Fun fact: When I was younger, besides wanting to be an "astronaut," I also dreamed of being a chief meteorologist on the local news channel. I was very interested (and almost obsessed) with weather, just like my dad, and I dreamed of being on TV. I also wanted to be a grade school music teacher, as I have been playing several instruments (specializing in piano) and singing since I was a young child.

The greatest lesson I have learned in my professional life is that no matter how hard or challenging a job may seem, if you continue to push yourself and keep an open mind and heart, you will be ready to learn. No day is the same as another. Although I have been practicing for six years, I still learn something new every day, and I will continue to do so until I retire. Every day is a learning experience, and it is important to frame that in your professional life. You will have a better work life satisfaction if you are ready to learn.

I am motivated by my community and my family. I realize that there are people out there who will always need my help. I know that I am able to provide that care to others, whether it's through my professional nursing care or through my personal life. My family is always my sounding board and they are also the reason that I keep going every day. I want to continue to make them proud by doing well in my environment and by helping others in my community.

My favorite quote is: "Be the change you wish to see in the world" by Mahatma Gandhi. I love this quote, as I feel that it is so powerful in so few words. I feel that every day it is so important to live with intention and humility, and to be open-minded and receptive to how you can help be a functional and useful person in society. Even if it's just as simple as showing a smile to another, you never know how much that will change somebody's perspective on their day or even their life trajectory. I hope that by becoming a nurse and now a nurse practitioner, that I provide this change on a daily basis. Although I may not necessarily see the reward of my actions daily, I rest easy knowing that I am making a difference by living with intention and purpose in some way every day.

There are plenty of memorable experiences in my career, especially working in the emergency department and in psych. It's tough to choose just one. There are definitely moments that I will never forget because they have made me stronger as a person. My most favorite moment was when I was still new in this department. I had a patient who ended up passing away. His wife was so grateful for the care provided. She could see that I was also saddened (as the patient was about the same age as my father). The next day, she came back with a card and some flowers. She gave me a big hug and told me how thankful she was for everything I did. I did not expect that at all, as it is my job to take care of my patients. It reminded me that I am a human being with emotions. It is okay to cry with your patients and express your feelings tactfully. I know that the patient's wife was grateful and I am so grateful for her too. I will always remember the patient and his wife. I still have the card in a keepsake box.

~Grace Ohm, Registered Nurse

I've always been inspired by my mom. She absolutely loves her job and has genuinely lived by the saying, "If you love what you do, you'll never work a day in your life." It's important to realize that life is too short to stay stuck in something that doesn't make you happy. Don't be afraid to explore and try something new. The grass isn't always greener on the other side of the fence but it might get you closer to where you truly want to be— whether you know where that is or not!

I'm a Registered Nurse Care Coordinator in Neurosurgery. I've only been in this position for about five months. However I've been an RN for nearly seven years in a variety of different roles including bedside ICU RN, case manager, cardiology clinic/cath lab nurse, and clinic nursing supervisor.

Having been in various types of nursing roles, I've learned that what I enjoy most about healthcare is working with a positive and collaborative team. It's when we, as a team, provide thoughtful and personalized care to patients and their families.

I really like the clinic setting. While there are challenges, there are also countless opportunities to learn without the stressfully emergent situations one typically deals with while working in an inpatient role. Clinic hours also provide a near-perfect work-life balance, which is something I find necessary in both my career and my personal life. To top it all off, I am fortunate that I have current coworkers that I have worked with in the past. That made me confident that I was joining a great team.

Even though I'm only five months into this position, I can already tell this is the best-fit job I've ever had. I've always wanted a job that makes me wake up excited to go to work. It took me a while – after having different jobs over a handful of years – but I finally feel like I'm happily settling into a role that I've wanted for a very long time. Without hesitation, I would choose this position again and again.

I have enjoyed aspects of my past roles, and I do not regret the time spent in those roles (nor do I regret leaving those roles, no matter how difficult it felt at the time). I believe in healthcare, and specifically in Nursing. There are so many wildly different roads one can take. Having a wide range of experiences inevitably enriches one's perspective, knowledge, and confidence as a healthcare provider. Personally, I was able to better determine my own strengths, weaknesses, and interests, so that I could pinpoint a position in which I could be successful.

It's okay, and even desirable, to try new roles, work in different settings, experience different healthcare systems as you build your career. If you're lucky to land a position you love right off the bat, that's wonderful! However, if you don't quite feel satisfied, or fulfilled, or happy in a role, do yourself (and your patients and team) a favor, and try something else.

I was able to identify and put together my favorite pieces of my different former roles to create an ideal position to pursue. I was able to use past experiences as a strength while interviewing for new jobs, and I also became better at "interviewing the interviewer" when deciding whether a new opportunity would be a good fit for me.

To further elaborate, for example:

Bedside ICU RN: This was my first nursing job out of college. I worked with an amazing group of nurses, physicians, and administrative leaders, and I learned so many important nursing skills, including the intangible ones like time management, critical thinking, and how to assert myself. It was also a neurosurgical-focused ICU. My love for working with neurology patients started here.

Inpatient rehabilitation case manager: I made this jump primarily because I wanted a regular Monday through Friday work week. I thought that I would better enjoy seeing patients recover and go home. Looking back, I had no clue what I was getting myself into, and while I quickly found out that it wasn't a great fit for me, I learned more than I ever thought possible about things like working with insurance companies and advanced directives. My coworkers were primarily social workers, so I also learned to deeply appreciate and collaborate with other disciplines in healthcare.

Cardiology clinic and cath lab nurse: Having spent time "behind the scenes" as a case manager, I wanted to get back to bedside care while also maintaining my Monday through Friday work week. I was terrified to transition to a new specialty (since my background was mostly neurology at that point), but I pushed myself. I liked the change of scenery and was able to split my week between seeing patients in clinic with the providers and providing hands-on patient care at an outpatient cath lab. I found that I excelled at providing patient education. I was able to build positive relationships with patients and their families, especially when I was able to see patients through the continuum from their initial consultation through their procedure and on through their follow-up care.

Clinic nursing supervisor: While I greatly enjoyed my role at the cardiology clinic, a piece of me persistently wondered about my place in nursing leadership. I had been a part of Nursing Shared Governance while working in the ICU. Since then, I had seen myself eventually assuming an administrative role in healthcare. I transitioned into a supervisory role of five busy – and growing – medical specialty clinics. In that role, I was lucky to have the incredible support of team-oriented coworkers and a manager who was consistent, straightforward, transparent, and vibrant – everything I wanted to be as a leader. I learned that I really enjoyed problem-solving and coordinating projects to improve patient care and team member satisfaction. My work-life balance became very imbalanced as I poured more of myself into the role, which ultimately led to me pursuing the position I am in now.

In my current role, I am able to provide patients with a clear picture of what their hospital stay after a surgery will be like. I have a better understanding of the complexities and intricacies of the healthcare system. I am able to help patients and their families navigate it through my experience as a case manager and nursing supervisor. Through all these past roles, I have learned the importance of staying nimble and open to tackling new challenges, especially ones that help me get where I want to be.

The most memorable parts of my career so far are not necessarily the experiences but rather, the people. The day-to-day challenges, struggles, and even successes do not compare to the amazing individuals I've had the honor to know and work alongside.

I'm motivated by my thoughtful, open-minded, and devoted team. The people I work with every day outwardly love their jobs and take pride in their work. It's easy to work together towards a common goal – providing great care to our patients – when everyone is "all in." I wholeheartedly believe that everyone cares for our patients and each other immensely. It's not difficult to stay motivated when I feel that positive momentum.

~Haylie Wargin, Registered Nurse

⸺⸺≻◈≺⸺⸺

I am a Registered Nurse. I have been a nurse for seven years. I always enjoyed Science and from a young age, I've always wanted to help others. If I could go back in time I would still pick a job in healthcare. But I would love to be a PA (Physician Assistant) in a Dermatology setting.

I've learned in my professional life to listen carefully to what others tell you. They may hold the key to the puzzle. A quote that inspires me is "Do not let yesterday take up too much of today."

My most memorable point in my career is when I saw my patient doing well after a critical stat call. Knowing that I am making a difference in the community and helping people to get through their toughest times motivate me in this job.

~Jackie Johnson, Registered Nurse

I've been a Staff and Stroke Registered Nurse on 1L Neuro ICU for almost five years. My friend in nursing school was a nurse extern here and told me they were hiring so I applied. I always thought I would be a Cardiac Nurse because that was my strongest area in school. I can't imagine working anywhere else!

My family motivates me in this job. They depend on me to keep going and I depend on them to keep me going. This job also taught me to always be nice to coworkers. You never know who will be your boss someday.

I especially enjoy the quote from the Dalai Lama: "Our main purpose on earth is to help each other and if we can't do that, at least don't hurt each other." Also, I always think about what my sister told me after I graduated. "Always treat people with kindness and respect because you never know what is happening in their personal life." I now keep that in mind daily.

I will always remember my encounter with a former patient. I thought he would be aphasic for the rest of his life because he had a left MCA (Mild Cerebral Artery) occlusion. But he walked in the ICU one day and asked to see me. He gave me a hug and thanked me for being there with him. He spoke in clear sentences!

~Jason Gallup, SCRN, Registered Nurse

I have wanted to be a nurse my entire life. I worked for one year as a bedside nurse and then transferred to the operating room for a change. After 30 years I was ready for a different challenge so transferred to the clinical research department.

I am currently a Senior Research Coordinator and I've held this position for almost 15 years. Before taking on this role, I was a Registered Nurse in the Operating Room for 30 years. I love my job and patients. I am fortunate to work with great physicians, hospital and clinic staff.

I definitely would encourage all high school age students to consider Nursing. It is challenging with many opportunities. There are not many jobs that afford the opportunity to work in the hospital setting, clinics, education, and informatics to name just a few options. I also had the opportunity at age 60 to go back for my BSN. I have learned that Nursing and Medicine are constantly changing with many challenges.

I am inspired by Winston Churchill's words: "We make a living by what we get. We make a life by what we give."

My most memorable experience in my career was when I was voted in as the Patient Care Nurse Excellence Award Winner. It was based on an experience I had in the operating room with a flight for life patient who expired. My communication with the family was also taken into consideration.

~Jennifer Cooper BSN, CCRC, Registered Nurse

I have wanted to be a nurse my entire life. I worked for one year as a bedside nurse and then transferred to the operating room for a change. After 30 years I was ready for a different challenge so transferred to the clinical research department.

I am currently a Senior Research Coordinator and I've held this position for almost 15 years. Before taking on this role, I was a Registered Nurse in the Operating Room for 30 years. I love my job and patients. I am fortunate to work with great physicians, hospital and clinic staff.

I definitely would encourage all high school age students to consider Nursing. It is challenging with many opportunities. There are not many jobs that afford the opportunity to work in the hospital setting, clinics, education, and informatics to name just a few options. I also had the opportunity at age 60 to go back for my BSN. I have learned that Nursing and Medicine are constantly changing with many challenges.

I am inspired by Winston Churchill's words: "We make a living by what we get. We make a life by what we give."

My most memorable experience in my career was when I was voted in as the Patient Care Nurse Excellence Award Winner. It was based on an experience I had in the operating room with a flight for life patient who expired. My communication with the family was also taken into consideration.

~Jennifer Cooper BSN, CCRC, Registered Nurse

"I've learned that people will forget what
you said, people will forget what you did,
but people will never forget how you made
them feel." ~ Maya Angelou

I have always loved this quote by Maya Angelou and I think about how much it relates directly with nursing and patient care. One of my favorite memories is when a patient returned to the unit to thank me. He remembered my face AND MY NAME. He told me that I was the best nurse he's ever had and that he and his family will never forget me for saving his life.

I've been a Registered Nurse for five years. After my husband and I went through the experience of losing our three children, my job at the time no longer felt fulfilling. I wanted to do more and be more. I felt pulled into nursing by that drive.

Nursing is a 24-hour job. You can't get everything done during your shift and you can't be perfect every day. You're still human.

My children are my motivation to get up and keep going. I strive to make them proud of me and to do good in their honor.

~Jennifer McGraw, Registered Nurse

I am a Registered Nurse and a Stroke/STAT responder. I have been in both of these roles for four years. I ended up in the Neuro ICU by chance. I knew that I wanted to work in an ICU directly after nursing school, but didn't know where. Prior to becoming a nurse, a physician I worked with referred me here after he randomly overheard me talking about wanting to work in an ICU. I got the job and never looked back.

My inherent curiosity motivates me to keep going. Learning never stops, and understanding this drives me to continuously educate myself so that I can provide the best possible care to our patients. I would never choose another job in Nursing. Neuro is my passion. However, if I could go back in time, I would want to go to medical school instead of nursing school.

The greatest lesson this job taught me is to be kind. The nature of our job never warrants being anything but kind to others. I believe in the general principle of treating others the way that I would like to be treated. You can't really lose with this approach.

My most memorable experience is a sad, but empowering one. I helped code a 35-year-old woman while her parents sat outside of the room and watched. Her parents were understandably very emotional as they watched a team of nurses and doctors try to save their daughter's life. Luckily, we were able to bring her back. On our way out of work that morning, her father hugged each of us and cried while thanking us for what we did. This was a very powerful moment for me. I think about it nearly every day that I work. It reminds me of the impact that we, as nurses, have on both our patients and their families. Most importantly, it reminds me that we see patients and their families during the worst moments of their lives. This empowers me to be the best that I can be and to always be understanding, compassionate, and kind.

~Jon Brockman, Registered Nurse

My official title is Julian Schuenke Registered Nurse and I work in the Neuro Critical Care Unit and the Emergency Department (ED) at Aurora St. Luke's Medical Center in Milwaukee, Wisconsin. I have been working in the NICU for about four years and the ED for about six months.

I chose to pursue a career in the medical field because I was influenced by various family member's professional roles in healthcare. I always aspired to have a career that directly and positively affects people's lives. Although many professions make positive impacts on people's lives, at the end of the day it is up to individuals to take care of their own health. Nothing is more important than your health.

I did not initially choose Nursing as a career. In my early high school and college days, I had my heart set on a career as a Physician Assistant. However, for various reasons I was unable to pursue that path. Although I had a college degree in Biomedical Sciences, I had no clear plan on which career path to follow. I contemplated giving up my goal of working in healthcare and going back to school to start over again.

Ultimately, I decided to pursue a degree in Nursing. My passion for working in the healthcare field and helping people prevailed, even if it meant starting over in a completely new career that I was not fully comfortable with at the time. If I could go back, I would have just become a Nurse in the first place instead of a Physician Assistant. I have a sense of fulfillment working in the ICU and ED as every shift brings new challenges. I am not exactly sure what I will be doing each day or what patients I will be caring for, but I know my work is important. Additionally, nursing affords many routes beyond working at bedside such as in management and research. In my case, I am pursuing higher education to complete my doctorate as a Nurse Practitioner to continuously grow in my profession.

The greatest lesson I have learned in my professional life is that sometimes you have to just let things go. You can prioritize what is most important and what you can get done at that time. When I started working in healthcare, I used to obsess over every finite detail of caring for patients and want to fix every problem they had during my shift. It was exhausting. I would end up staying late every shift trying to catch up with charting.

My first manager that gave me my first job as an ICU nurse gave me a valuable piece of advice. She reminded me that hospitals are 24-hour operations. There is always a next shift to take over because you cannot do everything on your own. I cannot fix every problem a patient has during every shift that I work. Everyone needs help and it takes a village to care for our patients.

Although I work a job dominated by science and objective data, what motivates me deep inside is faith. I have experienced my share of trials and difficulties in life. However, I am better and stronger because of them. I have been blessed with financial stability, good education, good health and most importantly, a family that supports me. In my eyes, this puts me in a position of responsibility to do something good with what I have been given. I was raised a Catholic and went to Catholic schools. The moral sense of right versus wrong has stuck with me and still drives many of the decisions I make to this day. In my gut, I know I am doing what I am supposed to be doing— caring for the sick— and that is what motivates me to get up every day and work such a physically and emotionally taxing job.

My mother always tells me when I have a problem: "If you don't ask, you don't get." While writing this entry, I looked up that PHRASE on Google and evidently it originates from either Mahatma Gandhi or Stevie Wonder. However in my brief search I could not verify either as the true source.

To me, that quote is about taking initiative in a situation when you could use some help. If you ask a person for assistance and you are turned down, at least you tried. However, if the person says, "Yes, I will help you," then you are in a better position than where you started with your problem. It does not hurt to ask for help.

As of this writing, the COVID-19 pandemic has been ongoing for months. I have encountered a fair share of COVID-stricken patients. But I helped care for an ICU patient that has created a bold imprint on my mind. He was intubated on a ventilator with inhaled nitric oxide to aide his breathing. We were intermittently proning him, to again aide his ventilation and oxygenation. He was on multiple sedation, paralytic, and vasopressor infusions to help with ventilator synchrony and maintain adequate blood pressure. We even gave him continuous renal replacement therapy, which is a type of slow dialysis, because his kidneys were not adequately producing urine.

He was a very sick man. Managing everything previously described is very labor intensive. Because of infection prevention guidelines, his family was not allowed to physically see him. Instead, the physician and I would call and talk to the family to keep them updated with the patient's condition. I cannot imagine not being able to be with a loved one who is critically ill like that patient.

The patient's daughter was a young school age girl. I would speak to her daily because she was the only family member that could speak English. The physician and I decided to set up a video chat so she and the rest of her family could see the patient. It took quite a bit of time to walk her through the set up on her phone and sync it with a hospital tablet device. This we successfully did while managing all the medical therapies as well. Only the video portion was working so I was on the phone with her at the same time. The physician and I then put on our protective equipment and showed her and the family how their loved one was doing. After describing all the medical devices in the room, we held the phone up to the patient's ear so his daughter and the rest of the family could talk to him. The young daughter was crying. What she said to her father I will not share, but in that moment, I was reminded of how special and impactful my role is in healthcare.

~Julian Schuenke BSN, CCRN, SCRN,
TCRN, Registered Nurse

I have been a Quality Improvement Coordinator of the Aurora St. Luke's Medical Center/ASLSS Practice Evaluation Committee for nine months. Prior to that I was a Heart Failure Coordinator for 10 months and Cardiovascular ICU (CVICU) Registered Nurse for 26 years.

I chose the CVICU job because I wanted a fast paced, quick decision making, challenging area where I could help optimize the patient's health through a holistic approach. I wanted to be able to perform those tasks while constantly learning and developing my practice and skills. I chose the Quality Coordinator position as it was time to transition to a more non-clinical role due to the wear and tear on my body over the years. I felt I could use my cardiac critical care knowledge to improve patient outcomes and provider performance.

Yes, I would choose each of these jobs again, and in the same order. The ICU position provided me with the vast knowledge base, attention to detail and interpersonal skills needed to be chosen for my current role and to perform that role at the utmost of my ability.

My greatest motivator is a sincere desire to help people in their health journey. I aim to improve outcomes and utilize my experiences to further educate and support my fellow healthcare workers, especially during challenging times, and there are many.

In this profession, you must have faith in yourself and utilize your resources. You constantly learn and support others through your learning and experience.

In the ICU, we confront death. In order to help cope, I found comfort in this quote: "Death is but a horizon and a horizon is but a limit to our sights." I also saw this on a billboard on a day I was particularly worried: "Worry is the dark room in which negatives are developed." I have remembered it to this day and passed it on to my patients. (Unfortunately, I do not know who to give credit to for these quotes.)

It is so precious to be a part of patient's lives in a meaningful way: the day-to-day emotion of taking care of the sickest of the sick, supporting them, celebrating success with them, crying with them, helping them stay alive and collaborating with them and their families through their process of death. Those are my most memorable moments in this career.

~Karen Sledge, Registered Nurse

I've been a Registered Nurse for seven years. My grandmother was a nurse and I saw how she made a difference in her patients' lives. In this profession, I discovered that every day you will be learning, and that things always change.

How can I make even just a small difference in a patient's life? That is the driving force that pushes me to get up and keep going at this job. "Just keep swimming." This quote from the movie Finding Nemo reminds me to keep going everyday through obstacles.

I don't have one memorable experience in my career that stands out. I have small ones in which I could get a patient to smile when they are going through a rough time.

~Kari, Registered Nurse

I've been working as a Registered Nurse Care Coordinator for the last eight years. However, I have been a Nurse for more than 30 years and my experience includes Neurology, Home Health, Rehab, Case Management, and Manager of a Medical Surgical Unit.

I like to say I did not choose to become a nurse. I always say it chose me. When I was 17 years old, my dad had a stroke and passed away. It was one of the most difficult times of my life. He was hospitalized several days before he passed, and I will always remember the great care he received from the nurses and doctors. Being an RN Care Coordinator allows me to help patients and their families receive the care they need. I aim to help them navigate the complex health system and provide education to help them maintain a healthy life and remain out of the hospital.

I would choose this field all over again. I was originally headed to college for law. I was working at the gas company when I was a senior in high school after my dad's death. One of the supervisors offered me an opportunity to go into the informatics field. In 1982, they called it the computer industry. I completely appreciated being offered the job but I informed the supervisor that I was going to nursing school. Sometimes I laugh when I remember that decision I made, but I know I was born to be a nurse.

Patients motivate me to keep going. It is usually something simple that they say or do. It's things like understanding and verbalizing to me that they know how important it is to take their medications, to weigh themselves, or to call the doctor when they experience certain symptoms. Recently one of my patients said to me, "This is your parole officer calling. My weight is 170 and my blood pressure is 130/70." He showed me he knew what to do and how important it is with his heart problem to monitor this weight and blood pressure. He made me laugh.

I love Nelson Mandela's quote: "Education is the most powerful weapon you can use to change the world."

Providing education to patients gives them the power to make informed choices about their health care."

In this profession, you're not just taking care of the patient. You're also taking care of the family. You also need to form a good relationship with the family and develop their trust.

There is no way you can be a nurse for 30 years not have so many memorable experiences. Recently, I was able to help a patient's wife make the decision to place her husband in hospice care. The patient had been declining for months. After having many conversations with his wife, I was convinced that she was just not ready for it. Then one day she called me. I will always remember her statement to me: "Lisa, as a Christmas present, I am going to put Jerry in hospice." I was stunned. I knew she had not been willing to let him go even though he was ready. For Christmas, she was giving her husband the gift of letting him go and allowing him a peaceful and quality end-of-life.

~Lisa Rusk-Nowak, BSN, Registered Nurse

I am a Senior Director of Quality Management Org 100. I have been a Nurse for 40 years. I have been a Staff Nurse, a Clinical Nurse Specialist Critical Care and was asked by the hospital President if I would take this job as an interim Senior Director of Quality Management. I accepted and ended up loving the job. I applied and was given the position.

I love being a nurse. I love every aspect of my career whether that is caring for patients and families, mentoring and teaching newer nurses, changing nursing practice to reflect "best practice" or currently tracking and trending data to improve patient care.

The greatest lesson I've learned in this professional life is that a "title" does not give you respect. You have to earn it.

I have never forgotten what it was like to be that "new" nurse right out of school, caring for my first patient or calling that first physician. Every day I work to make a difference for our patients.

"If you do nothing more than what you did yesterday, you will never have anything more than what you have right now." That is a quote that inspires me.

My most memorable experience was working for a Patient Care Manager who believed nurses were independent thinkers and decision makers. She stood behind each of us. She expected the best from her nurses and every nurse on that unit looked professional, acted professional and was proud to be a part of her team!

One day she told me I was an excellent nurse and I did a great job caring for the most difficult high acuity patients. However, she was not going to give me a raise that year because I was not involved in any committees. She explained to me that part of professionalism as a nurse means being involved in decisions that are made regarding the care of our patients. I was not happy and thought about her words.

Approximately four months later, I joined a Nursing Practice Committee where we reviewed and approved nursing practice decisions, policies, and products used on patients. It was the best thing I ever did in my career because I found that as a "staff nurse" I did have a voice! I became more involved and over the years became a Clinical Nurse Specialist in Critical Care and completed my PhD in nursing.

I continue to work every day for the patients and have been at my site for over 30 years. I also teach nursing part time as my passion is helping nursing school students identify their interests and successfully transition from student to staff nurse.

~Mari St. Clair, PhD, Registered Nurse

I am a Registered Nurse Medical Assistant Consultant III. This job is with the Office of Inspector General. I review physician billing for Medicaid fraud. I review records for quality of care, potential risk of harm and excess or unnecessary care and billing Medicaid. Most of the physicians in these cases have been suspended or on probation.

I think Compassion is what Nursing is all about. Never ever take anything for granted. The circle of friends I have is something people will never get. The love we have for each other is a crazy, fun sisterhood. We have grown up together from having weddings, to babies, to divorce, to funerals and now to Cancer. Through it all we have all been there for each other. This is a bond like no other.

Here are some simple thoughts but truly inspirational: "Be yourself. Be kind. Tomorrow is not a promise. Every day is a new beginning. Smile and enjoy every moment. Life is too short. You have a job to do and if you must, have some fun along the way."

~Mary Richey, Registered Nurse

For five years, I've been a Registered Nurse. Prior to being a Nurse, I was a Veterinary Technician, then a Dental Assistant. I chose to go into Nursing because I love Health and Medicine. I have already gained medical knowledge and developed patient care skills. I wanted to get into a well-paying career.

I have come to realize I love Microbiology and fixing stuff. If I could go back in time, I might choose to be a microbiologist who works in a research lab, or an appliance repair person.

I have learned I cannot make assumptions about where others are coming from or what they know. Making these assumptions leads to miscommunication. I have also learned that it takes a special kind of strength to care for people when they are most vulnerable. Not everyone can be a nurse.

I hear from patients that they appreciate me and that I've helped them. It feels good to do good for others. I know that nurses will always be needed and this job will allow me to provide for my family. I also know that I can always learn more and develop in my career.

This is from a song by The Roots that often rolls through my head: "You don't say 'good luck.' You say 'don't give up.' It's the fire, inside you. Let it burn." I think about this when someone is going through something tough. Don't hope for good luck because luck is never a sure thing. The only person you can and should always be able to count on is yourself.

When I open my mind up to special memories, many flood in. There are so many brief moments that have stuck with me such as listening to James Taylor with a dying woman, singing "Roll Out the Barrel" for a patient who was a huge Brewers fan, and coming together with my fellow nurses to care for a crashing patient. When I think about what these memories have in common, it is making connections with others.

~Melanie, Registered Nurse

———————

I have been a Registered Nurse for five years. I enjoy caring for critically ill patients and find it rewarding. I also love working with Neuro/stroke patients.

Here are some words I live by: "Never give up, no matter how hard it gets." My coworkers, patients, and my family all motivate me to get up and keep going.

You will make mistakes, but you will always learn from them and they will make you stronger. That's what this job has taught me.

I had a transplant patient who got another chance at life. He had such a good spirit and drive to do the best he could. That was a memorable experience for me.

~*Melodie Kriefall, Registered Nurse*

<hr />

My job title is House Supervisor at St. Luke's South Shore hospital. I have been a nurse for 17 years. I chose this profession to challenge myself and learn more. I am also a single mother and I wanted to show my daughter that a woman can take care of herself without having to depend on others. If I could go back in time, I would still choose this job. I have learned so much and met many great people in this career that I would never want to change it.

The greatest lesson I have learned in my professional life so far is that mentoring is important for the next generation of nurses.

My family is my biggest motivator. They are the reason I get up and keep going.

A quote that inspires me comes from my mom. When I was young, she would always say "Do unto others as you would have them do unto you." I have made that quote my own by saying that I treat others the way I would like to be treated or would want my family to be treated.

The most memorable experience in my career was saving my uncle's life. I convinced him he needed to go to the hospital as I could tell that something was not right with him. I had a feeling that he had some type of infection. My uncle had developed pneumonia that progressed to sepsis. Had I not gone to his house that morning after work and convinced him to go to the hospital, he would not be here right now.

~Micki Campbell, Registered Nurse

⟫●⟪

I am an Emergency Department Registered Nurse. I have been a Registered Nurse for seven months, but I have worked in the Emergency Department for nearly four years. I started off as an Emergency Department Technician while I was in nursing school. During my last year of nursing school, I also worked as a Nurse Extern. I graduated from nursing school eight months ago, and began working as a Registered Nurse one month later.

During my childhood, I was raised by parents who dedicated their time to giving back to others. Volunteering and giving back to my community was not a choice; it was a responsibility and something that I quickly grew to love. I knew that I wanted to dedicate my career to giving back to others, and I was intrigued by the healthcare profession. It gave me the opportunity to give back to others every day. I ultimately chose the Nursing field because I knew that I wanted to spend time with my patients and gain the one-to-one interaction with them. Nurses are known to be "the most trusted profession" and during my time in the healthcare setting as a child, nurses have always stood out to me as the kind individuals who have made me comfortable. After speaking with multiple nurses, I knew that nursing would be the perfect career for me.

I love speaking with others and getting to know new people. I also love staying busy and "staying on my feet." Because of this, I knew that the Emergency Department would be the perfect, fast-paced setting for me. Not only would I constantly be busy, but I would also have the opportunity to meet new individuals on a daily basis.

Not only do I absolutely love what I do, but Nursing also offers great flexibility, in terms of schedule, opportunities, and specialty.

One of the greatest lessons I have learned in this profession is to enjoy the simple pleasures of life. Often times, our society becomes distracted with work, school, politics, and other worldly diversions that we forget to enjoy life. It is important to take a break, read a book, walk by the lake, and enjoy spending quality time with family and friends. Mental health is crucial. It is important to realize when to take a mental break to recharge and reenergize.

My patients and future patients keep me going. Working in an Emergency Department allows me to meet new individuals every single day, and new challenges and experiences motivate me to come to work every day. I truly enjoy coming to work because each day is a new experience and a new challenge. The interdisciplinary team that I have the pleasure of working with also motivates me, as they continue to teach me (as a newer nurse) and assist me in reaching my highest potential. Coming to work and being part of a dedicated team motivates me to be the best nurse that I can be.

I have two quotes or verses that I live by and both come from the Quran, the holy book in Islam. The first verse is found in Chapter 20: "Oh my Lord, increase me in knowledge." I believe it is my duty to continue to seek knowledge, whether medical or about various religions or cultures and other topics. In my opinion, furthering education is crucial and necessary.

Another verse that inspires me is in Chapter 5 of the Quran: "Whoever saves the life of one person, it is as if he has saved all of mankind." This motivates me to provide the absolute best care for my patients.

I am unable to pinpoint one specific memorable experience in my career, but those that stand out are related to the phenomenal teamwork displayed by my coworkers. All team members – nurses, physicians, techs, and other staff members— are able to count on one another during some of the most difficult, emotional, and intense situations. My team is strong and resilient, and that is demonstrated by staff members able to go back and forth…with ease… between patients, from the very unstable to the stable. Throughout all of the difficult situations we may face, the team always comes together to help each other while caring for our patients. After spending nearly 13 hours per day, three days a week with the same individuals, a very special, unique bond is created that is indescribable. In healthcare, after experiencing many crucial and demanding moments, our coworkers quickly become family. We are able to depend on one another in ways that are challenging to articulate.

~Nisreen Atta, Registered Nurse

I have always had an interest in medicine and the science behind it. I am also a people person and I like to socialize and make relationships. That's why I went to bedside nursing. I've been working for three years as a Registered Nurse.

I would definitely choose this job again! I love meeting different people and getting to know them in what is usually the most vulnerable time in their lives. This job has humbled me. It has made me grateful for what I have, made me appreciate my relationships outside of work even more, and it has given me an opportunity to meet new people and help them through tough times. I am pursuing Nurse Practitioner (NP) school because I desire more education to help my patients.

The greatest lesson I have learned is to always be honest with yourself, your colleagues, your patients, and in your life. Being honest has allowed me to develop as an individual. I have come to accept my strengths and limitations for what they are. I have gained respect from other colleagues. I have been able to be the voice of reason and comfort for patients with my honesty (especially as most patients don't like things sugar-coated). All of these outcomes have taught me to be honest with my lifestyle and with who I am. These little lessons have affected my life choices, and I have become a much happier person since.

My motivation to get up and go is the continued learning process. I love the science of helping and healing patients. Every day that I go to work is another day of new exposure and a new opportunity that helps me grow.

"You're darned if you do, and you're darned if you don't." I live my life by that. You cannot please everyone, every time. So if something makes you happy (and is safe), go for it!

My most memorable experience in my career is probably when I got trained into the ICU and developed the confidence to apply for NP school. I was a floor nurse for two years prior to this. I would have NEVER dreamed of coming to an ICU. I decided to challenge myself when I started looking for a new job as I was moving to Milwaukee from up north. I have trained in the ICU. I have challenged and pushed myself to be a better care provider than the day before. Now, only a year later, I am getting ready to apply for Nurse Practitioner school! Woo hoo! I would have NEVER had the confidence to make such a leap before this job. I finally woke up one day and said "I have the confidence to become an NP." That moment was pretty darn memorable for me.

~Paige T-Grover, Registered Nurse

I am a Registered Nurse. I graduated from Northeast Wisconsin Technical College in December 2016 and have been working as an RN since January 2017.

I chose this career path because three of my aunts are Registered Nurses. I have always had a passion for Math/

Science and caring for people. My drive to take care of people comes from my Catholic faith and Jesus' message to care for the sick and carry out the corporal works of mercy.

If I could go back in time, I would have chosen the exact same career and education path. I am so grateful for all my great mentors and the experiences I have encountered along my Nursing journey. I'm still so new to the field!

For me, the greatest lesson I've learned was how to collaborate with a team. Before Nursing, I was accustomed to relying solely on myself to get things done right and on time. But through the years, I have become much better at working with others. I've become a better teammate in facilitating successful patient outcomes.

I thoroughly enjoy working with the Interventional Radiology (IR)nurses, techs, and doctors. Everyone in the department is so friendly and willing to help me whenever I have a question or need assistance when the department is busy.

My favorite quote comes from my favorite NCAA basketball coach, Bobby Knight. He said, "The key is not the will to win...everybody has that. It is the will to prepare to win that is important." Preparation takes so much discipline. I believe it is the people that go home and truly evaluate their work ethic, approach to studying/

preparing, and finally their execution in the workplace that sets them apart.

My most memorable experience was when I was working in Green Bay at the Brown County Community Treatment Center. A patient was admitted for psychosis. It took about 3-4 weeks before this patient was stabilized and finally discharged. Prior to discharge, the patient made me a paper origami heart that I still keep with me. The patient told me that despite her psychosis, she remembers how well I took care of her.

~Philip Marchi, Registered Nurse

I'm a Registered Nurse (RN). I have been a nurse for 24 years. I graduated as a nurse in India and have worked in different countries like India, the Middle East, Ireland and here in the United States.

To tell you the truth, I chose this profession so I can start working as soon as possible. Right after high school, I went to Nursing school and earned my degree at the age of 20. I was very happy that I started earning in my 20s.

The Nursing school I went to was a Christian institution. They taught me the importance of empathy and the meaning of compassionate nursing. That changed my opinion on what a real nurse is. There were times my feelings were hurt by some ungrateful and rude human beings. I have met some patients who treated nurses as slaves. I didn't give up, though. I got a lot of respect as a nurse when I started working in Europe and the United States. I believe this is the job filled with humanity. We become one of the family members of the sick patient. We spend most our time with them and we wipe their tears. The respect, love, and blessing we get from this profession is enormous. I believe there is no other profession that can provide the same. I have been an ICU nurse for more than 15 years and I've cried along with the ones in critical condition. I learned a lot being an Cardio Thoracic ICU nurse for the last seven years. I consider myself a very confident nurse.

I feel like I have born in this world to be a nurse as I have spent more than half of my life as an RN. I don't know If I can do any other job other than being a nurse. I might become a nurse instructor to prepare good nurses. The love I can share with my family, friends and my patients keeps me going.

The greatest lesson I've learned is that human life is temporary. The purpose of human life is to serve, to show love and compassion, and to have the will to help others as Albert Schweitzer said. This is my motivation. I also want to be kind to everyone around me.

There are a lot of memorable experiences I've had in this career. One that I still remember is when one of my patients sent an inspiring story book to her daughter before leaving this world. Even in her last days, she did not forget to send her token of love. Recently, a patient with a Tracheostomy hole in his neck came to convey his thanks to each and every one. He underwent ECMO treatment for more than a month. He was grateful for getting his life back. I can still see the happiness in his face, his wife and little kids.

~RN, Registered Nurse

My current job title is RN Case Manager in Utilization Review. I've been in Case Management since 2017. I have held several positions immediately after graduating from Nursing in 1993: Medical/Surgical unit at Queen of the Valley Hospital; Perioperative Surgical Services; Cardiothoracic Surgical team in Pomona Valley Hospital Medical Center (Heart Team); Cardiac Catheterization Laboratory Holding Unit; Charge Nurse in the Cath Lab Holding Unit at Riverside Community Hospital. After getting my Bachelor of Science in Nursing degree, I changed jobs entirely and moved into Case Management.

I really wanted to be a Physician originally. I went to Cal Poly Pomona with a major in Biology/Pre-Med. My grades were not competitive enough for Medical School, so my counselor suggested another pathway. My girlfriend's mom at the time was a Registered Nurse. I decided to pursue the Nursing route instead. It turned out to be the best decision.

Being on the Heart Team at Pomona Valley Hospital was my most memorable and formative time in my career. I learned a lot about teamwork. Anticipation. Adaptation. Grit. Perseverance. Critical thinking.

I want to care for and protect people. At my core, I'm a protector, a sheep dog. A Nursing career was a perfect fit for me with my gift of serving and caring for people.

If I were to go back in time, I would more than likely end up in the same profession. Even if not in the same capacity, it would still be in Medicine. I probably would have joined the Military and pursued a career in medicine there, whether as a physician or a Registered Nurse, Physician Assistant or Nurse Practitioner. But I chose my current career path through the love I have for my girlfriend at the time. She is now my wife of 26 years. I know would have married her again.

The greatest lesson(s) I have learned are that God gave us two eyes, two ears, and one mouth. With this in mind,

I know that we should see and listen twice as often as we should speak. Everyone has a story. Everyone has a perspective. I believe everyone at their core is a good person. Understanding where people are coming from and trying to understand them with empathy provides a greater avenue for effective communication, compassion and community.

I have been knocked down many times in my life. I have fallen off the horse (so to speak) and started the race all over again. I have learned to live through the trials, failures, tribulations as a means of navigating life. I have also learned to hop back up on the horse from where I have fallen off so as to not relive prior mistakes.

What gets me going everyday is knowing that I can make a difference in someone's life. I can plant one little seed that may benefit someone in some way. Throughout my day every day, I try to make a difference by providing for my family or through interacting with the people I work with. Knowing that God gave me a gift, I willingly oblige with sharing my gift with everyone around me.

I have a personal quote that I made up: "Life is a never-ending educational process. One could never know enough. One could never know too much." Another quote that I live by is from former Navy SEAL Jocko Willink, "Leadership is not one person leading a team. It is a team of leaders, up and down the chain of command, working together to lead." This is the foundation of teamwork. No one person is better than the other. Each person, in and of themselves, is a leader. Each is capable of stepping up to follow as well as stepping up to lead where needed. When someone tells me that there is no "I" in team, I would have to step in and tell them otherwise. What would a hand do if it didn't have its arm? What would a foot do if it didn't have its leg? Each piece is an integral part of the whole.

~ Robert "Bobby" Gonzales, BSN, Registered Nurse

I will always be a Nurse. I have been a Registered Nurse for 29 years. I love my job. It's the only job I know how to do. It's the only job I know that is spiritually rewarding.

In this profession, my family motivates me to keep going. They inspire me every day. When I care for the elderly, I see my Mom in them.

I believe in doing your job from the heart. It makes it easier and more enjoyable.

Life is precious and it ought to be treasured. Life is fragile and it ought to be cared for. We must live life to the fullest with our loved ones and family as life is only borrowed. It has its time frame.

There are plenty of memorable moments to mention. Some are funny, some are sad, some are joyful. As a nurse, I was given an opportunity to see the joy of life from birth, and at the same time see the sorrows when life ends.

~Rosefil Aguilar Dindin, Registered Nurse

⟞⟡⟞

I enjoy it when patients that I have taken care of in the ICU walk into our unit and say hello sometime after discharge. It is pretty cool to see the strides they have made after recovering from strokes or bleeds.

The greatest lesson I have learned in my professional life is to always treat people with respect and empathy. You never know what kind of day a patient or a coworker might be having. You just don't know what could be going on in their home life.

My wife motivates me to get up and keep going. She is an extremely hard worker and when I am feeling lazy, her persistent and determined mindset makes me feel like I need to hold up my part of the bargain in our relationship.

"Life's a garden...dig it." This is a quote from a movie called Joe Dirt. To me this quote means you are responsible for your own destiny. Your actions are met with consequences. If you work hard, make good choices, and learn from your bad choices, you will be happy in life.

I have been a Registered Nurse for six years. I enjoy working with people and attempting to put a smile on their face. It was always my lifelong dream to be a professional hockey player so if I could go back into time I would pursue that. If that didn't work out, I would still be a nurse.

~*Ryan Peterson, Registered Nurse*

———————

This profession has taught me that we are all the same. We meet people when they are vulnerable and need comfort, care, and understanding. It can be very overwhelming at times, but it's rewarding. I've been in health care for 37 years. I was a Licensed Practical Nurse (LPN) from 1983-2011. I've been a Registered Nurse after that.

Frankly, I was tired of factory jobs. A friend told me I would make a good nurse. I've never thought of pursuing a career in Nursing. If I were to go back in time, I would have become a Registered Nurse immediately, went on to take up Masters and taught Nursing after years of experience.

These are the quotes that help me daily:

"This too shall pass."

"The Lord will never give you more than
you can handle."

I gain satisfaction from a job well done and making a positive impression on someone who is going through illness.

The most memorable experience I've had in this career was crying with a patient who just had a heart transplant. Patients that die in my care are always with me.

~Sandra Lee, Registered Nurse

———— ❊ ————

I am a Director, Professional Services & Senior Consultant, MD Review and I've been doing this job for 22 years. I started as an Administrative Assistant in a medical staff office and have grown into the position where I am.

Assume the best in every intention and move on. This is the greatest lesson my professional life has taught me.

My most important motivation is improving the quality of care my organization offers to patients.

My favorite quote comes from the movie "A League of Their Own": "It's supposed to be hard. If it wasn't hard, everyone would do it. The hard is what makes it great."

I will always remember the time I assisted a provider who had a substance abuse issue. I was able to support him in seeking the right help. He was able to return to his profession and patient care without compromising his career.

~Sara Cameron, CPMSM, CPCS, Registered Nurse

"Growth is painful. Change is painful.
But nothing is as painful as staying stuck
somewhere you don't belong."
~ Mandy Hale

I have been a Registered Nurse Specialty Care Coordinator for Epilepsy for a year. I worked inpatient as a nurse for two years prior to taking this role. I started to feel comfortable in my role as a floor nurse but wanted a new challenge, so I chose this new position.

I really miss bedside nursing and face-to-face interaction with patients, but I have also developed an ongoing relationship with our regular patients which I love. I would probably still have chosen to take this position, but I do sometimes wish I would have ventured into critical care.

I think the greatest lesson I've learned in my professional life is that you are in control of it. Your actions guide your future. If you have a certain goal you want to achieve, only you can make that happen.

I have found a passion for this career that I never knew existed. Being a nurse is not only my job, but part of my identity. There are constant challenges and opportunities for growth. I also care about the patients – they're what keeps us all going.

There isn't one experience that stands out to me. But finally finding the confidence and comfort in my practice—stepping into leadership positions, being trained as a charge nurse, precepting other nurses— is what I consider my most memorable moment. It felt good to be able to relate to newer nurses while being a resource for them. I enjoyed being able to share my knowledge with them.

~Sara Ebsen, Registered Nurse

I have been a Registered Nurse for almost four years. It is the greatest profession ever!

Ever since I was young, I wanted to help people. I have a love for serving others. I enjoy Medicine and learning about the human body.

This is a quote that inspires me to embrace my job:

> "Act as if what you do makes a difference.
> IT DOES." ~William James

Each day, my patients and co-workers motivate me to get up and keep going. I know my patients rely on me and need me. That motivates me to show up every day and be better every day. My co-workers motivate me because they always bring a positive light into my life, and encourage me to be better.

The greatest lesson I have learned is to treat everyone equally and with dignity. Everyone comes from different backgrounds, and we have to care for each patient as though they are our very own family member.

My most memorable experience in my career has been training/precepting new nurses. I found such joy in being able to patiently watch them blossom into excellent nurses. I enjoyed sharing my knowledge with them, as well as helping them learn new things with me along the way.

~Savanah Nicarlo, Registered Nurse

I am a Registered Nurse Care Coordinator for the Neuro Vascular team at Aurora St. Luke's Medical Center. I've officially been in my position for three weeks, but unofficially in this position for the past 11 months.

I was fortunate that I obtained a Licensed Practical Nurse (LPN) job within the outpatient clinic. I later transitioned into a Medical Scribe role. I scribed for multiple specialties over two years and fell in love with the patient population within the Neuro Vascular world. I felt like I had such a great opportunity to learn from the physicians in this department. They also seem to be the most caring group of physicians I've had the pleasure to work with. A combination of a love for the patient population, the enjoyment of learning the specialty, and a great relationship with the physicians made it an easy decision for me to try to get my current position as a Care Coordinator. I feel like I've been groomed for this position. I owe it to the patients and I also want my children to grow up seeing their father excel in his career.

If I could go back in time, I would have earned my degree sooner and become a floor nurse in the hospital first to gain more general experience. With that being said, it isn't a feasible option for me right now to do that with my young family. I need to balance my work and personal life, which this position affords me.

These are the lessons I've learned in this profession:

Hard work pays off. Character matters more than skill. Skill can be taught over a short period of time but character takes time to develop. It is important to focus on becoming the right type of person rather than just aiming at getting things right.

If I had to choose one memorable experience, it's probably when I was an LPN working with patients during their final days and hours of life. I've really enjoyed being present with family members during some of the most intimate and difficult moments of their lives. It's truly been an honor. I know that this isn't my current role, but it is what is most memorable.

I lean on this quote to guide me: "Only one life 'twill soon be past. Only what's done for Christ will last." -C.T. Studd

~Shane Engen, Registered Nurse

⸺⸻⸺

Healthcare isn't a job that you choose. It's gifted to you. In this lifetime and the next, I would choose a career in Nursing. This career allows me to serve my community and be a motivational leader that empowers those around me to advance healthcare. What motivates me is knowing that the job is never done, and patients are depending on us to show up and be excellent.

I am currently the Nurse Supervisor for three of the ANII (Aurora Neuroscience Innovation Institute) Clinics. I have been in this position for four months and I have been part of the Advocate Aurora Family for four years.

A career in healthcare is a journey. That journey assisted me to understand the core of choice in serving as a Registered Nurse and now as a Nurse Supervisor. In my nursing and leadership journey, I have met nurse leaders that poured into me, pushed me, and motivated me. They highlighted my qualities, making me aware of my ability to be successful in my nursing practice and as a nurse leader. Also, my mentors drove me to become a positive influence for my team members who may not understand their own potential. I am only great because of my team and I win when they shine. I chose this job because I believe in excellent care for our patients. I lead by example and I hope to inspire others.

The most memorable moments in my career are those times when my leaders and colleagues trust in my ability. That facilitated self-growth, which led me to do the same with my team members. Self-actualization promotes growth and confidence, creating positive outcomes for our patients.

Here's what I have learned. The power is not in your title. It's in the ability to see from someone's else perspective.

Here are some quotes that give me inspiration:

"Sometimes I inspire my patients; more often they inspire me." ~Unknown

"The best way to find yourself is to lose yourself in the service of others."
~Mahatma Ghandi

~Shrenka Lazzari, Registered Nurse

———»•«———

"Too often we underestimate the power of a touch, a smile, a kind word, a listening ear, an honest compliment or the smallest act of caring, all of which have the potential to turn a life around."
~Leo Buscaglia

This is a quote that in my opinion summarizes why nurses and doctors touch the lives of so many. It's not just the science, the surgeries, and the medicines. It's us as people. It's the in-between moments when we listen and reassure. I think this quote encompasses why I love my job so much. All those small things really mean the most to so many. I feel so blessed and grateful to God that I am able to be that person who uses my knowledge and my gifts to help others in such a manner.

I am a Registered Nurse on a Cardio Thoracic Surgical Transplant Unit at Aurora St. Luke's Medical Center. I'll be at the hospital for nine years this coming October. For six years, I've been a nurse. From a very young age, the medical field and sciences have always interested me. I knew that one day I would work in the medical field in some way.

I feel very blessed to work in this position. To be able to help patients and family members at their most vulnerable is very humbling. Without knowing anything about me, these people trust me implicitly. For that, I will always show up to work ready and willing to help ease their worries, help keep them safe, healthy, and on the road to recovery.

I do not think I could do anything other than work in the medical field. I actually switched from Pre-Med to Nursing. The Inpatient Nursing world is where my heart lies. I feel very blessed to be working so closely with the patients and other healthcare providers.

I love being able to learn new things that keep my nursing skills sharp and discover new ways to help my patients. I have learned so many valuable things throughout my career. Always trust your gut and listen to it. Always advocate for your patient's well-being no matter how unpopular that may be at the time. Never be afraid to ask a question. It will keep you wise and prepared.

There truly has never been a day that I dread going to work. Simply put, my patients and my coworkers motivate me. Do I wish I had holidays off? Sure. Do I wish I could sleep in some days? Absolutely. But do I feel grateful every day to wake up, do a job that I love, and work with people that I admire and respect? Without question, 100% yes.

There is nothing I wouldn't do to help keep my patients safe as well as my fellow coworkers. I just know that if everyone helps out and does their part, it will make everything run smoothly. That's why taking care of patients is really a TEAM effort. It is all the different specialties of doctors and nurses that help care for the patient and all of us doing our jobs and communicating everything we learn both effectively and in a timely manner.

Off the top of my head, I cannot think of any specific quotes that inspire me. But I do know that I personally refuse to fail and I will always give my all. I grew up with a single mom of four. My mom did everything and anything to make us feel safe and loved. I have that same work ethic.

~Sonia Bista, Registered Nurse

I am a Registered Nurse II. I have been a nurse for almost four years. This job helps me make a difference in people's lives— whether in big or small ways. I've always had a passion to help others, I'm fascinated with Science, and I want to keep learning. Nursing fulfills all those for me.

During my early college days, I doubted my Nursing course so I took up Public Health. I later pursued a Master's in Public Health with a concentration in Epidemiology. I wanted to do Infection Control. Post grad school, I was having a very difficult time finding a job since everyone wanted a Nursing degree for Infection Control. I started to look back into Nursing and it became apparent that this was the right path to take. I've thought about switching to something else or a different aspect of Nursing, but I still feel a strong pull to continue doing what I'm doing.

In Nursing, there are so many options, paths to take, and areas to get into so you can keep learning and developing. I've really grown to feel like I'm a part of something. I've gained new experiences and have become a teacher and leader. I couldn't imagine doing anything else.

When I was taking my Master's program in Indiana, I did an internship in Indianapolis' public health department in the TB unit. The staff worked with a lot of refugees from Burma. I saw the nurses' passion as they helped the refugees obtain their necessities. That inspired me to build a career in Nursing.

I also gained a deeper love for this job during the pandemic when our unit was a COVID unit. Our patients were not able to have family members or a support system at the hospital, so the nurse became the patient's and the family's support and voice. I really began to feel that I was making a difference, that I was becoming an advocate and a source of hope for the patients and their families. It was perhaps the hardest thing nurses have ever had to go through.

I think the biggest thing I've learned is to trust your gut. Your gut is usually right, even if you may not physically see something wrong at the moment. Trusting my gut has saved patients more times than once.

I'm motivated to get up and keep going knowing that each day is a different day with different people and different situations. I love the variety. I work second shift and I work with a pretty great group of people who make work fun.

I really like this quote from Steve Jobs, "Your work is going to fill a large part of your life, and the only way to be truly satisfied is to do what you believe is great work. And the only way to do great work is to love what you do."

To be a nurse, you really have to love what you do and believe that you are making a difference. I strive to make each person's day brighter, even if it's a minimal way. I came up with "Each day is a new opportunity to brighten someone's day and put a smile on their face even on the darkest days."

Here is my most memorable experience in my career:

We had a patient that had been in the hospital for about two months. It was around Christmas time. We reached a point where there was nothing more that could be done for this patient. I already knew this patient from a prior hospital stay but got to know her more during this time. I also got to know her husband and their family through everything. Although the situation was extremely heartbreaking, I was amazed at how the patient and family were taking the news with such positivity. In such a time of darkness, they were doing everything they could to make each day the best day for all of them. We all saw a sign of strength that changed us on some level or another.

~ Stephanie Carpenter MPH, BSN,
BC-CV, Registered Nurse

I am a Registered Nurse in the Neuro ICU and I have been in this position for just over four years. I chose to get into healthcare because of my aunt. She was a Registered Nurse in the OR. She loved her job and constantly talked about how amazing being a nurse was. She died about eight years ago from a ruptured brain aneurysm. At the time, I was a Nursing Assistant in the PACU/SDS but I had no plans to continue my education. After my aunt's passing, a patient went out of her way to tell me she believed I would make a great nurse. I don't know why but it just hit home. I just remember hearing my aunt's voice telling me to continue pursuing a Nursing career. I made it happen and was in school within the next year.

I would definitely choose Nursing again. I get a lot of fulfillment out of my job. Every day, I feel like I make a difference. I enjoy coming to work. Nursing has taught me many things but the most useful are learning patience and remaining calm. I try not to get overwhelmed by things that are out of my control.

I think getting into healthcare requires someone who understands that there are good and bad days. Unfortunately, when it's bad it can get really bad. But, for me at least, discussing the bad situations with fellow nurses and knowing that they understand how I feel, is really helpful for me to get over the bad times. I know I can always count on my co-workers and I know I can trust them with my life. I don't think other careers can say that and I don't' think many people can understand the relationship between healthcare team members.

I try to keep in mind that even though I do this everyday and it's routine for me, most of the people I come into contact with are having the worst day of their lives. If they are short with me or rude, I never lose my temper. Instead, I try to figure out how to make their day just a little bit bearable. It could be as simple as giving them a warm blanket or playing some music. It is amazing how just a little kindness can change someone's day.

One of my most memorable experiences was when I lost a patient unexpectedly. The patient was older and just had a procedure that caused her to bleed out. I remember working for hours and hours trying to get her BP back up. We gave boluses and started 3 pressors. We intubated, started multiple lines, and attempted to get a CT but ended up losing a pulse. I had an orientee with me and it was her last day on orientation. The whole situation was overwhelming but the thing I remember most was that the oldest son was in the waiting room the whole time. I had a few discussions with him about stabilizing the patient and he could come in once things calmed down. Unfortunately, they never did and we ended up having to call a code. When he heard it, he came right away to tell us to stop as the patient wouldn't want to be resuscitated. We then started comfort measures. After the patient passed, I ran up to the son who was on his way out. I just told him how sorry I was for his loss and asked if there was anything else I could do. He just gave me the tightest hug and said, "Thank you for everything." He said they were ok and that this is how the patient would have wanted to go. I was devastated and felt so guilty for not being able to save the patient. But knowing that I did right by the family is all I can ask for. I cried all the way home that day.

~Stephanie Serkowski, Registered Nurse

———➤●◄———

I'm a Care Coordinator Registered Nurse working for Aurora Neuroscience Innovation Institute (ANII) the past five years. I started off as a Licensed Practical Nurse (LPN) then earned an Associate Degree in Nursing (ADN) and now I'm a Bachelor of Science in Nursing.

In the beginning, I chose this job because of the hours. But I stayed because of the patients and co-workers. Also, I like the free education I've gained from seminars and meetings.

I would choose this job again. The support from management really surprised me. When together you continuously see patients due to their illness, bonds are created. My co-workers make the difficult times seem easier. We support each other and there is so much laughter. I would not want to change that.

My family, helping people, and seeing progress— all these motivate me. The greatest lessons I've learned in this profession? Never give up and it's okay to ask for help.

I experienced memorable moments here at ANII while working in ENT, seeing patients at their worst and watching the stages of the healing process.

"If you are going to dream, dream big!" That's a quote that I find inspiring.

~Tammy Albiniak, Registered Nurse

⟶ ≫ ● ≪ ⟵

I've been a Registered Nurse for 26 years. When I was about five years old, I watched a TV show called Emergency. I loved it and wanted to be Nurse Dixie.

I probably won't choose this job If I went back in time. That is if I could retain the knowledge I have now. I would love to be a wildlife rehabilitation specialist.

These are lessons I've learned in my life as a nurse: Expect the unexpected, and most of the time it pays to really listen to your patients.

My motivators? My love for the job mostly. And then there are the bills!

The most memorable experience in my career was from my ER days. I had the opportunity to save the life of an 18-month-old little girl.

My favorite quotes:

> "To thine own self be true." ~William Shakespeare's Hamlet That's one of my favorite quotes. The other one is from John Lennon's song: "Imagine all the people living life in peace."

~Tina Klotz, Registered Nurse

My title is Lead Registered Nurse, Intrathecal Pump Program. I've been doing this for about two years but I've been a Registered Nurse for almost 12 years.

I chose to be a nurse after an experience I had with nurses that really made a difference for me! I had neck surgery (spinal fusion) at age 32. I was so nervous to let someone cut into my neck. I was afraid of what it would mean for me in terms of pain, healing, and lifestyle. Even the surgery itself concerned me. Would I wake up when I was supposed to? But my nurses were so amazing. Prior to the surgery, they talked to me about what to expect, and eased my anxiety.

After the surgery, they pushed me just enough to keep me healing well. At one point, when my blood pressure dropped and I almost passed out, they quickly got me into a safe position, started some fluids, and got me feeling better right away. I realized that it was the nurses who really made a difference with the patients. Doctors are great. Surgeons fix the mechanical stuff. But the nurses? Nurses are right there with the patients, talking through the fears, teaching, helping, encouraging, and empowering. When a person is about to "go down," it's the nurses that do the interventions to help make that person feel ok again!

That whole experience really made me want to be a nurse. I wanted to be able to help people the way they did— like the way they helped me! I thought I was too old to start nursing school at that time. My family used to ask me, "Why don't you just do it?" After a few years of my family encouraging me, I finally did it. I went to Nursing school part-time while continuing to work full-time. While it was a challenge, I never considered quitting. I was so inspired to get out there and make a difference in the lives of people in need. I graduated from Nursing school at age 40.

I absolutely would still choose this job if I were to go back in time. I love being a nurse! I cannot think of anything I would rather do! I was an inpatient nurse for about five years, an Emergency Department nurse for almost five years, and now I've been the Lead for our IT Pump program for about two years. Each position taught me so much. Each also had its challenges, but I wouldn't change a thing.

I have learned that we should never judge anyone. We have no idea what a person is going through. If there's something we don't understand about a person's behavior, it's probably because we're just missing part of their context. In my role as nurse, my job is to compassionately care for every patient as much as I possibly can. That's it. No judging. I can teach patients in the hope that having a better understanding of their own health might help them make healthier choices. Even if they don't, I have to reserve judgment and just meet each person where they're at, and treat them compassionately.

Helping people motivates me. Sometimes it's hard to get out of bed, to get moving. But I think about our patients, the needs they have, the questions they have, their fear and/or anxiety. All of that is what gets me up: my desire to answer their questions, calm their fears/anxieties, and help them find ways to meet their needs.

"Be the change you wish to see in the world" (attributed to Mahatma Gandhi, I'm not sure if he ever actually said it.) There's so much pain and suffering in this world. I wish that were different. This quote reminds me that my part in that is to BE different myself. I try to be merciful and compassionate, and to see the best in people. I think if we all could truly do that, the word would be a better place.

This might sound strange. We spend so much time trying to save people. This is especially true when I worked in the Emergency Department (ED). So much of our efforts were all about keeping people from dying. But one of the most memorable experiences I had was with a woman who was dying in our ED. She knew she was dying. She was a DNR and she was at peace with it. She had strong faith and believed she was going somewhere better, after dying here. When her monitor alarmed because her heart rate was slowing dangerously, I was able to be by her side. I held her hand and reassured her. She looked so peaceful as she took her last few breaths and began her eternal rest. The peace of that moment will stay with me forever.

~Tracy Lopnow, Registered Nurse

I want to have an impact on people. It gives me great satisfaction to enhance someone else's journey.

I'm a Registered Nurse and a Bachelor of Science in Nursing Patient Care Coordinator. I manage the intake of cranial neurosurgery patients. I have been doing this for almost seven years. Before that, I was an inpatient nurse on an orthopedic/med surge unit for two years.

I am grateful that my life led me to a career in Nursing. It combines my love of teaching with my desire to continue to learn. I feel like I learn something new or meet someone new every day! The people I work with inspire me to be my best and I would not change a thing.

My most memorable personal experience was finishing nursing school when I was 38 years old. I had a part-time job, three children, and I commuted over an hour to every class. It was a satisfying achievement that has paid off with a rewarding career!

My undergraduate degree was in Speech and Hearing Science. I thought I wanted to be a Speech Pathologist when I was in elementary school. I completed the course and earned my degree but decided I was more interested in teaching. I had taught piano lessons in high school, so knew I liked teaching children. Later, I completed my Masters in Elementary Education, certified K-6.

Life then blessed me with my husband, three children, and several dogs! My husband's job moved us to five different states: Wisconsin, Minnesota, Arkansas, Indiana, and Connecticut. During that time, I taught in several different classrooms while mostly focusing on raising our children. When we got back to Wisconsin, our children were all school-aged and I wanted a full-time career. The school system in Wisconsin was going through government changes at that time which made getting a job in that field difficult. That's when I decided to return to school for my Nursing degree. Nurses need to be excellent teachers, so it felt like a good fit for me.

After working on an inpatient unit and gaining solid experience, I was fortunate to join the Aurora Neuroscience Innovation Institute in its earliest stages and help develop the program. It's been rewarding to help this population of patients and work with amazing and gifted surgeons.

"Let's turn good ideas into good plays." I overheard a parent say this from the sidelines while I was watching my daughter play basketball. People always say, "good idea" when players try things and it doesn't work out. Turning that good idea into a good play needs practice and effort. You need to work hard to make things happen.

This profession has taught me to never stop learning and improving. ALWAYS be a good listener. Every patient has a different story and needs an individualized approach.

~*Tracy Rothwell, Registered Nurse*

⋙●⋘

"We are what we repeatedly do.
Excellence, then, is not an act, but a habit."

I'm a Registered Nurse working in the Neuro ICU as a Bedside Nurse and a Rapid Response/Stroke Nurse. I have been with Saint Luke's for eight years. Growing up, I had a few injuries as a result of playing ice hockey which led to my initial exposure to our healthcare system. I never was afraid of the doctor but, was intrigued to learn more about my injury and plan of care. This experience led me to pursue a career in Medicine.

Knowing that I can make a difference in someone's life is by far my biggest motivator in Nursing. It may just be another day for me but for a patient, that day could be the most terrifying experience of his or her life. By simply showing kindness, I am able to help reduce their fear.

I have learned over the years that if there was ever one organ that we could say houses the human soul it is the brain! You can get a transplant of almost any other organ from another person or have a machine temporarily take over for those organs but the brain is individual to you and you alone. It makes you who you are. There is no such thing as a brain transplant and there are no machines that can run your brain. As a nurse working in the Neuro ICU we are protecting someone's damaged brain and literally saving their soul.

Recently, I took a patient outside and gave him a haircut. This patient had been in the hospital for a month and had not been outside once during that entire time. He was a stroke patient who made it to rehab, but further complications brought him back to the ICU. I had the pleasure of speaking to him on the phone after he got home. He told me how grateful he was for giving him the hope and motivation he needed. I thought I was doing a simple task but he said that act of kindness completely turned his outlook around.

Presently, I have been caring for a 53-year-old father of two. He is critically ill due to COVID. He has made improvements in the past two days but he is still very ill. I really hope he gets better. Taking care of a COVID patient is physically and mentally exhausting but knowing that what I did during my 12 hours with him gives him the best chance at survival— a chance that his kids may still have a dad— gives me a strong feeling of purpose.

Being in this profession has taught me that life is short. Be grateful for what you have. There are so many people going through far worse things and to get upset over something small is not worth it.

~West H Bauman, Registered Nurse

CHAPTER 20

Occupational Therapists

I entered undergraduate school studying Biology with the intention of applying for Veterinary school. I always gravitated towards Science throughout grade school and junior high. I thought I could combine my interest with animals into a career. While working as a Veterinary Tech, I realized I really enjoyed educating the owners about their pets' conditions. I decided to transition to an Athletic Training degree to focus on human health. During my senior year, I interned at a sports medicine clinic and fell in love with the clinic side of rehabilitation. After completing my undergraduate school, I went to Occupational Therapy school, focusing on orthopedic injuries, and here I am today working as an Outpatient Occupational Therapist. I have been in this role for almost six years.

I go back and forth between Physical Therapy and Occupational Therapy. I like that Outpatient Physical Therapy can treat more areas of the body versus Occupational Therapy. However, I also enjoy that Occupational Therapy has allowed me to specialize in specific surgeries of the elbow, forearm, wrist, and hand.

This job teaches you to get comfortable with being uncomfortable (especially in the beginning of your career). You can never know it all and you'll encounter challenging diagnoses and patients. Just use it as a learning tool to progress your knowledge and practice.

Frequently people ask me if I get bored with my career because I encounter similar injuries and diagnoses. I don't. The body is an intricate thing and there is always something else to learn. In the same note, every patient is different. The way they respond to their injury is unique to them. What motivates me is finding out the best treatment techniques to treat an injury while discovering the best way to make the information/rehabilitation relatable to the patient.

While I was a student, my clinical instructor told me, "Don't be the clinician you were last year." Keep growing in your knowledge. I like to apply that same thought on a personal level too.

I remember working with a patient who suffered a severe fracture in the forearm requiring extensive surgical intervention. She arrived at her therapy evaluation very tearful and frightened, with limited functional use of her arm. Over time, the patient became less fearful and began to show progress in motion and strength. By discharge, she was crying happy tears because of how far she had come. She was finally able to hold her grandchild comfortably and confidently again. That was a memorable experience for me.

~Anonymous 1, Occupational Therapist

———⋙◉⋘———

I've been an Occupational Therapist for 21 years.

My grandmother had a fall and fractured her arm. I took her to therapy and saw how the Occupational Therapist treated her. The focus wasn't just on her broken arm and the function of her elbow joint. It also focused on how the injury impacted her functional tasks and daily living. I related to this holistic focus of her treatment. That's why I chose this job.

> "Life is not measured by the number of breaths you take, rather by the moments that take your breath away." ~Unknown

You can see tragedy and triumph all in the same day. The human spirit is amazing, and people can defeat the odds. Some days are going to be great, while other days suck the life out of you. It's about finding balance and focusing on gratitude to maintain a positive mindset.

Every day is a new day, another chance to impact the people I come in contact with. You never know whose life you are going to change. That's what keeps me going in this job.

One of the most memorable experiences I've had was caring for a patient with necrotizing fasciitis. He had lost so much tissue and muscle and really had to re-learn how to perform basic daily tasks. He lost entire core muscles (Latissimus Dorsi) and portions of his rectus abdominus were resected. He had to learn core stabilization with what remained after numerous debridement, as the team tried to stay ahead of the bacteria.

He was a young husband, father and avid softball player. The reward in caring for him came with small victories as he regained independence. The greatest memory was when he came back months later to the acute care setting, walking independently without any assistance or device. He thanked us for our efforts in helping him during his early treatment days when he was so sad and angry about his functional loss.

~Anonymous 2, Occupational Therapist

I have been an Occupational Therapist for about 12 years. My family motivates me to get up and keep going at this job. I chose this profession to help people live a better life.

Everyone has a different idea of quality of life that we, as healthcare professionals, need to take into account.

I believe in the statement: "Take it one day at a time" — for patients and for myself.

In general, discharging patients who have been in the ICU for a long time are wonderful memories for me.

~Beth Crespo, Occupational Therapist

CHAPTER 21

Onboarding Representative

I'm a Clinical Office Assistant/Business Office Lead but I recently changed positions. I am now an Onboarding Representative within Talent Acquisition, working remotely from home. I have been in this new position since January 2, 2022.

I chose this new position so that I could continue to grow with the organization. Instead of relating to our patients, I now relate with our new team members in the pre-boarding stage of their employment. It's great to be able to help them and answer all their questions. We are setting the first impression of the organization for these new hires.

If I could go back in time, I would probably go with my initial career choice which was to be a teacher. Life happened and things didn't work out that way. But I have been able to put myself in situations where I am able to work alongside children. I get the biggest kick out of them.

The greatest lesson I have learned is to be honest. I also learned to be a leader, to show others integrity and be the example.

My children are my big motivation. I always want to set a good example for them, whether it be at home, at work, or at play.

"One day at a time. Don't look forward and don't look back. Be in the present." These are the inspirational words I live by.

I have such fond memories of clients/patients and the relationships and friendships that have been forged throughout my career. The conversations, the kind words, the hugs, and even some tears along the way are among my most memorable moments.

~Heather Rude, Onboarding Representative

CHAPTER 22

Opthalmic Technician

My job title is Ophthalmic Technician I and I've been doing this job for almost eight years—about two years at Aurora and almost six years at a private clinic. I kind of fell into this position. I initially started as a Clinical Office Assistant (COA) at a private clinic and quickly moved up to insurance coding and billing. That didn't keep me as busy as I was used to, so I took it upon myself to learn the Tech function. I found that I thoroughly enjoyed the patient care and direct contact aspect of it as well as learning new and challenging skills.

I really wanted to be a doctor. I had all the grades and the drive for it. Then, life happened and cultural pressure took over. I come from a family that has a "work hard" mentality associated with physical labor versus educational advancement for success. Cultural expectations were also a contributing factor. After some very difficult losses, I dropped out of high school and consumed myself in work to provide for myself and help my family. If I could go back, I would not allow my family to dictate my future. I'd keep pushing hard for my own dreams/goals versus what my family wanted of me. I am now planning on pursuing my Bachelor of Science in Nursing degree in the fall.

Inspirational personal quote: "From mistakes to greatness, let that be your story!"

Original quote: "You have to consciously decide and believe that you deserve to feel free, that you are deserving of your dreams coming true. Do this with so much love in your heart and self-appreciation, and break through your life's barriers, so that you wouldn't want to do it any other way.

I believe that everyone has a story. Everyone has their "why"— positive or negative. So, remember this: Start each day with a kind, caring and grateful heart. May it be reflected by your work and bring light to someone else. Also, don't allow others to put you down. Prove them wrong with your own success and positivity.

I may not have a spouse or my own children, but I have my siblings and their children. They are the reason I keep going. They very much deserve inheriting my success for being my greatest encouragement. I also very much love doing everything that I can to help with someone else's journey of healing— no matter how short or long, no matter how easy or difficult. Being a helping hand or voice brings my own heart joy and peace.

I've got to say that I've had many memorable experiences, good and bad. However, there is not one that particularly stands out to me. I do look forward to having many more in the future.

~Martha A. Jimenez, Ophthalmic Technician

CHAPTER 23

Patient Image Assistants

I'm a Patient Imaging Assistant. I applied for this position because I thought it would be very interesting to work in the Radiology Department, learn how to do IVs, and become more knowledgeable about what goes on inside the human body.

Yes, I'd choose this job again if I were to go back in time. I learned a lot especially working with nurses and techs, but I would probably do Surgical Tech.

I learned to take care of myself and my family. This job also taught me to be grateful for what I have and appreciate life in general. Other great lessons I learned include being adaptable to change, and always keeping a positive attitude and outlook in life. Don't be negative and always go above and beyond.

My family keeps me motivated, and so do my team members and patients. They all play a big role in my life and I am sure I play a big role in theirs. I come to work every day to provide for my family and to help save lives. I want to make sure that my patients feel comfortable and aware that we are here to help them have the best experience under our care.

This is a quote that inspires me: "If you have the power to make somebody happy, do it. The world needs more of it."

The special memories I have from this career come from building special bonds with outpatients and making them feel welcomed. I had one patient who had been around since I started. Everyone knew him. I ended up building a bond with him over the months the I took care of him. He recently passed away which was very sad. But just being a part of his journey, giving him the best patient care, and being a friend to talk to about sports is something I would always remember.

~Desirae Rosado, Patient Imaging Assistant

For 22 years, I've been an Imaging Assistant for CT with Aurora St. Luke's Medical Center.

I wanted to be part of a team. I love the benefits Aurora offers. I also love the stability of a bigger company. For these reasons, I chose this job.

I have made lifelong friends here with my co-workers. I feel appreciated here. I learn new things all the time and love the patients.

My professional life taught me the great lesson of respecting my coworkers and really know how to work as a team. Teamwork can make or break your day.

My family and the fact I wake up healthy every day...those are my motivating factors.

Faith in God is my biggest inspiration. He will always get you through the tough times in life.

There was a holiday season when I was having a rough time with money. My coworkers came together and surprised me with Christmas gifts for me and my family. That brought me to tears! I was so happy to see how people really cared in my CT department.

~Sara Tapia, Patient Imaging Assistant

CHAPTER 24

Patient Service Representative

I have been working as a Patient Service Representative for 15 years. I was referred for this job. If I were to do things over, I would have been an elementary school teacher.

Prayer is what keeps me going in this job. Meeting wonderful people is the best part.

This profession teaches you to be more understanding. Patients come in from many different reasons. Some are mean (but not trying to be) because of their illness. Being kind and patient seems to win them over. We never know what a person is going through.

My quote is: "It is what it is." Most times you can't change things. Take it as it is and do the best you can with what you have.

~*Anonymous, Patient Service Representative*

————>•<————

Whether it was going to lunch together and talking over Diet Cokes, just working and being around Gail was like a miracle in itself. Gail was truly an authentic disciple who, quietly as an angel, shared her many talents and love with all those who encountered her. I'm very proud to have had such a supportive friend with strong convictions and one who stood up for me and others. Gail always believed in me, even during the times I failed to believe in myself. I'm very blessed and thankful for what a gift "Gail" was to me and others. Because of Gail, I have become a better version of myself. The miracle came late, though. It arrived on the morning of Gail's funeral. Besides being her best friend, I discovered that Gail was my distant cousin. I love all the memories I have of Gail and I pray that Gail continues to guide me and all those she cared about during her journey with us while here on Earth. This truly was the most awesome and memorable experience I've had while working at St. Luke's Hospital.

My second memorable and unique experience out of many that happened here at St. Luke's is that of being in the right place at the right time. While outside at the main entrance of the hospital, a couple pulled up in their car to the Emergency Room. I ended up delivering a new healthy baby daughter before I could even help the mother out of the vehicle.

I currently serve as a Patient Service Representative II in the Patient Access Admitting Department. I've been in this role now for 10 years. I'm happy and proud to say I have been employed here for 29 years.

Being analytical and trying to have an eye for detail are two reasons why the position "chose me." Now, why did I choose this position? I love my faith and I want to use my ability to serve others through their many different challenges. I feel the goodness that comes with helping others.

While I gained much knowledge and expertise in past careers, I would choose to stay in this current position that I love. If the option of going back in time did exist, I would maybe do something differently to see if I'm able to change and impact the future in a more positive way.

Quotes that tend to inspire me are: "Decide to lead and choose not to follow!" and "Always have faith. Trust God and keep believing."

My first motivational factor is the faith and knowledge in God. It is God who gives me life daily, my breath, and everything that makes me complete. Additionally, I'm motivated by my earthly treasures of home, work, pets, charity, church as well as the people and items I care for.

Some of the greatest lessons I have learned begin with having faith and believing in miracles. This first one is incredible and with some prayer and hard work, it truly works. The second lesson is to always treat others well. Be a good leader by example and have others do the same for you. Some challenges come with the second lesson because the other person may not always be kind. But we must be patient and stay steadfast. We should strive to always treat them with sincere kindness because they might not have experienced this kind of love in their life. Third lesson is to tell the truth and have the courage to do it and know it.

~Brian J. Neal, Patient Service Representative

Chapter 25

Patient Transporter

I gave someone a warm blanket. It is just a small gesture but to explain in words how happy he was for it would be impossible. That truly was an amazing feeling.

I've been a Patient Transporter for five years. I enjoy helping people as much as I can. It also gives me the opportunity to meet new people. This job helped me grow and learn many new things such as enhancing my listening and communication skills in any environment.

I wake up every day knowing it is a new day and to not only make my life better but those of others as well.

When I think about inspirational words, what comes to mind is my friend Arlene. She always tells me to "never give up."

~*Sladana Bjelanovic, Patient Transporter*

Chapter 26

Pharmacists

I've been a Pharmacist for 20 years and have always enjoyed science and healthcare. What keeps me going is being able to contribute to patient care and knowing each day will be different.

It is important to help patients understand their medications and simplify their regimens when possible. It is also important to learn to communicate effectively with various people (nurses, doctors, students and patients).

I was involved in a lengthy life-saving emergency for a hospitalized patient. The care team was very dedicated and we had gone through many rounds of medications in an attempt to keep the patient alive. She was found to have a pulmonary embolism. The patient survived and was transferred to ICU. A few weeks later, I delivered prescriptions to the patient's room. To speak to her and her daughter was truly humbling and gratifying.

These words of Ralph Waldo Emerson stay with me: "Do not go where the path may lead, go instead where there is no path and leave a trail."

~Anonymous, Pharmacist

My title is Clinical Pharmacist. I have been a pharmacist for 20 years.

As a young woman, I liked helping people and I felt that it was a higher calling. I was a Medical Technologist in the Microbiology Laboratory prior to returning to college. I wanted to use my previous education in my next profession. Pharmacy was a good fit for me.

I think it was one of the best decisions that I have made. When I graduated, I did not realize how my job would change. I really enjoy monitoring ICU patients and rounding with the ICU team. I love helping patients and my coworkers. In this job, I am motivated by my children and the patients that may need help.

The best lesson that I learned was the importance of continuing education. I became board certified in Pharmacology and Critical Care over the last seven years. That requires rigorous continuing education. I believe this has really improved my practice.

It is hard you me to choose my favorite quote, but I really like the quote by Johann Wolfgang van Goethe: "Whatever you can do or dream you can, begin it. Boldness has genius, power, and magic in it."

~Kerry Koloske, Clinical Pharmacist

CHAPTER 27

Phlebotomist

I am a Phlebotomist II Ambulatory Float. I have been a Phlebotomist for 11 years. I chose this job because I was unsure of what I wanted to do in the future. I didn't want to go to school and let it be a waste. One of my high school teachers had suggested this for me. She told me to get my foot in the door and explore the medical field from there. I loved working with people and helping them was an even better feeling.

I love my job but I really wish I went straight for my Nursing degree. I have been trying to complete my Nursing degree for years but it is hard to have to work full time and go to school full time.

This job taught me that being kind and compassionate will get you a long way. Even if others aren't kind to you when you are kind to them, it really changes a lot of situations. What motivates me to keep going is knowing that test results give doctors and patients answers to a road to recovery. Every sample is a life!

I have always been strong about treating any of my patients like my own friends or family. I want what is best for all my patients because I would want all my loved ones getting the same treatment! I have always shared that with other co-workers who may not have the same mindset. That has always helped people to do their job efficiently and promptly.

When I worked outreach, going to other people's homes, we would do a lot of tasks other than just drawing blood. I would always help like take out the garbage or be a listening ear when needed. I know I ran into some crazy situations. One instance was when my patient was having a seizure. I called 911 and then sat with him the whole time, making sure his head was safe. I waited until the paramedics arrived and made sure he felt safe until I left. If I experienced anything like that, I would want someone to do the same for me.

~Melissa Anderson, Phlebotomist

CHAPTER 28

Physician Assistants

I have been a Physician Assistant for eight years. I wanted a career in the medical profession and I enjoyed the flexibility of being able to change specialties without having to go through a new residency.

The importance of communication is the greatest lesson I've learned in this profession. When working as a team, communication is key to providing the best care possible to our patients.

The ability to make a difference in the lives of my patients and their families is what makes me get up and keep going.

One of the physicians I worked with at my previous job told me that no matter how bad of a day you are having, never take it out on your coworkers. Always try to work with a smile and a positive attitude. I have tried to mirror this in my own practice. I have found that by working with an upbeat attitude even when I am having a bad day, changes how people interact with me. It can even turn my own mood around.

Having a patient and their family thank me for my care and support during a difficult time in their lives is one of my most memorable experiences.

~Anonymous, Physician Assistant

Neurosurgery was a new specialty for me. I was nervous to start something completely new. But it was also a challenging field that allowed me to participate in surgical procedures. I have now been a Physician Assistant for Neurosurgery for two years. If I could go back in time, I would get a medical degree.

No job is perfect, but you make the best of what you're faced with. Learn from it to become a better person, colleague, and provider. Many things can be improved with good communication.

In the words of Rumi, "Only from the heart can you touch the sky." This inspires me and my colleagues motivate me.

One of my most memorable experiences in this career was convincing a homeless patient that their life is worth living. I was able to talk the patient into resuming chemotherapy after giving up treatment due to depression.

~Nancy, Physician Assistant

Chapter 29

Physicians

Stroke is a disabling disease, quite often affecting patients who are in the prime of their life. Having the ability to help them, especially in the acute setting to make the most difference in their outcome, is very satisfying. That is why I chose to become a Neuroendovascular Surgeon. I've held this position for a year.

In my profession, I have learned to interact with humility and respect.

We have patients who come in, unable to talk or move due to blood vessel blockage in their head. When we are able to help relieve that blockage and the patient starts talking and moving, the joy we experience is unparalleled.

It is heartening to see so many different people pulling together to take care of an individual. My most memorable career experience is working as a team to be able to give a patient the best care, like getting a room ready while ensuring patient comfort in the middle of the night.

My favorite quote is: "God helps those who help themselves."

~Anonymous 1, Physician

I believe in pouring your heart and soul into everything you do for the greatest benefit to others.

I'm a Clinical Cardiac Electrophysiologist and I've been doing this job for six years. This is an interesting and challenging job. Believing in the work I do is what gets me up and keeps me going.

The best outcomes often occur when the patient meets the doctor halfway. Medical innovations help in saving patients' lives and also improve quality of life.

My most memorable moments are when I'm able to make my patients and their families smile.

~Anonymous 2, Physician

Every smile of a patient and their family becomes memorable for me. Although we cannot help cure every patient, we can help them and their family suffer the least.

I've been a Cardiologist for 18 years. When I was young, everyone who studied well in my country often chose to study as a doctor. But now I think it's destiny.

Inspiration and faith from my forever King Rama IX of Thailand are what keep me motivated. I believe in purifying the mind according to the teachings of the Lord Buddha and doing your best.

~Anonymous 3, Physician

Margaret Thatcher said, "Watch your thoughts for they become words. Watch your words for they become actions. Watch your actions for they become habits." I find this quote inspirational.

I chose to become a Physician/Neurologist as I was interested in how the brain works. I wanted to help people afflicted by diseases of the brain. I have been doing this job for 10 years. If I were to travel back in time, I may still choose the same profession with an emphasis in teaching or I might choose the field of education.

The greatest lesson I have learned in this profession is to keep on challenging myself. Making a difference in the patient's life motivates me and keeps me going. For me, there is not one memorable experience. The ones that I recall are when I come up with a diagnosis when the signs/symptoms were not consistent with the physical exam.

~Anonymous 4, Physician

———————

"What fears you endured from evils which never arrived." ~Ralph Waldo Emerson

I believe this means you should not worry about things over which you have no control, but always do your best. I've been a Professor of Medicine in the Division of Cardiology for 30+ years.

I wanted to teach young doctors how to care for patients in an environment where I could also care and have a relationship with my patients.

What keeps me motivated is the joy of knowing that what I do will be passed on through my students long after I am gone. There is a great deal of satisfaction in seeing your students go on to achieve their dreams, whatever those dreams may be. You always hope that they remember you fondly and appreciate the efforts you made on their behalf.

The greatest lessons this profession taught me are patience and tolerance.

~*Anonymous 5, Physician*

———➤●◄———

My career choice was a bunch of smaller choices combined. I chose to be a Physician to try and use my scientific mind to help people in a very practical way. I became a Neurologist due to a fascination with the workings of the brain. I chose to study movement disorders based on having many pleasant interactions with patients with these disorders. I've been a Movement Disorders Neurologist for four years.

I know my patients would suffer if I did not keep working hard to support them. People value being listened to and truly heard. If you can make a patient feel like someone has heard them, that goes a long way toward healing.

In this career, I will always remember a special experience I had. Our team was able to help improve the movements of our patient with Parkinson's disease to a point where he completed a terrain race. The whole Parkinson's care team attended the race and participated in it with him. I will never forget him crossing the finish line and the sense of pride we all had in his journey.

~Anonymous 6, Physician

⸻⸻⸻

I have been a Neurosurgeon for 29 years. I completed my training in 1991.

This job chose me. I thought it was the most challenging, mysterious discipline in medicine. The Neurosurgery residents and attending physicians I met during medical school were bright and funny. I just wanted to be part of it.

The greatest lesson I learned in this profession is to never stop learning from your successes and failures.

"Patients first" is my only mantra. There is work to be done, questions in need of answers, suffering in need of solace. That is why I keep going at this job.

What is the most memorable experience I've had in this career? For me, it is the chance to be part of the lives of patients and their families facing a truly life-altering illness. I am grateful and humbled that I can witness their grace and courage.

~*Anonymous 7, Physician*

I'm an Associate Professor (Physician) at a University Hospital in the US, and a Professor in Thailand. I chose this job because of the research and the social contribution opportunities. If the core values in life are met, regardless of the place/type of work, then I can keep going. This includes doing research, helping others and traveling.

The greatest lesson I've learned is to pay it forward. Take one step at a time but don't stop. To me, the most valuable item is time. When you spend time with someone, the person in front of you is the most valuable person.

In this profession, my most memorable experience is working in Thailand with a team of health care professionals contributing to diabetes care.

~*Anonymous 8, Physician*

"Make a difference." Those inspirational words have helped me in my profession. I am a Family Physician. I was interested in Medicine and there was a shortage of doctors around my home so I pursued this career path.

Given the chance to go back in time, I would choose this career again. However, all the electronics that go with it now aren't my cup of tea. I would remain an independent practitioner.

My patients are what motivate me to get up and keep going. In this profession, I've learned that all parts of your life are important. Try for a balance.

~Anonymous 9, Physician

I love my job and wouldn't pick a different job. I have been a Neurointensivist for seven years. I chose to sub-specialize in Neurocritical Care during my Neurology residency because I really enjoy taking care of the sickest people in the hospital. I like the fast pace and immediate feedback I receive when I am managing a critically ill patient. I also enjoy the ethical issues involved in caring for patients in the Neurocritical Care Unit. Lastly, I get a tremendous amount of satisfaction in saving lives.

The very first day I was an intern, I helped save someone's life during a code blue situation. I will always remember that experience.

Unfortunately, it's not the quality of medical care that a doctor provides that determines if they are successful, but rather their interpersonal skills. I have a strong sense that I am able to provide exceptional care that patients will otherwise not receive if I am not taking care of them. That's what motivates me in this profession.

My dad once told me this and it helps me during tough times: "Worrying doesn't accomplish anything except wasting your time and energy."

~Barak Bar, Physician

I am an Endocrinologist/Internist. I work in a private hospital and also work part time (teaching and supervising residents and fellows in endocrinology diabetes and metabolism) at a government hospital. I have been doing this for 16 years.

I actually didn't know what I really would like to do when I was young. In Thailand, we have to choose the faculty for the entrance examination right after high school. I chose Medicine as my family supported me in doing so. Then I chose Endocrinology as my father has many endocrine conditions like metabolic syndrome, diabetes, and dyslipidemia. I also like the way endocrinologists work. As endocrine condition is usually chronic, we get to follow our patients for a long time. This way, we get to know the person well that they become our acquaintance, our friends.

I found out when I was in my thirties that my passion is to live in harmony with the earth and nature. I then tried to find the way to do so in my career life. As an endocrinologist, I spend a lot of my time talking to patients about how they live their lives. Therefore, I have an opportunity every day to help people live in the way that is better for them and also better for the planet.

This profession has taught me to find meaning in every little thing that you do so you could do it with much love. What motivates me is knowing that I could do what is meaningful to me even if it is just a simple, small act.

I live by these words of wisdom: "Live in harmony with nature and help others to be able to do so." I think this quote (my version) is a mix between the words of Thich Nhat Hanh and Jane Goodall.

I remember many small events throughout this career that brought me joy:

- I remember looking at the sunshine in my examination room in the morning before I start my day with gratitude.
- I remember my patient with dysphasia, trying to tell me about the little gift that she brought me. Her husband told me afterward that she had to practice saying it many times before coming to my clinic.
- I remember my patient, who came in the clinic feeling stressed and depressed, telling me he felt understood and encouraged at the end of the visit.
- I remember the joy that I had when my patient showed me the picture of healthy food that she cooked.

~Chorthip Nartsupha Pattanasri, Physician

I am a Neurosurgeon. I started residency training in 2004. I have been at my current position since 2015. I chose this profession because the brain is cool and I like to learn new skills and technology. In Medical School, the nervous system was the organ that I knew I would want to spend the rest of my life studying, due to both its challenging complexity and that there was so much yet unknown.

In Medicine, I would definitely choose the same specialty. If I wasn't in Medicine, I would design and build furniture.

This is a quote that inspires me to take action: "Never doubt that a small group of thoughtful committed citizens can change the world; indeed, it's the only thing that ever has." ~Margaret Mead

I have skills that can change someone's life and I feel a responsibility to use them daily for good. This motivates me to get up and keep going at this job.

The first time someone thanked me for helping a loved one to die well was a memorable experience for me. Quality at the end of life is becoming more important to patients and their families. We only have one chance to get it right for each patient, and it is a lasting gift we can give to the family.

The greatest lessons this professional life has taught me are: that life is uncertain, people are complicated, and love is powerful.

~Juanita Celix, Physician

I have been a Neurologist for 13 years and an Interventional Neurologist for six years.

I fell in love with Neuroanatomy class when I was a medical student. Our nervous system is very fascinating and I was lucky to have a brilliant neuroanatomy teacher, Dr. Techatat Techasane. He inspired me to become a neurologist. I like the challenges of making a diagnosis for patients with neurological conditions. It really requires a solid knowledge of neuroanatomy.

I chose the subspecialty of Interventional Neurology because I saw my mentor, Dr. Sophia Janjua, save many stroke patients' lives emergently. Some of them recovered and were back to normal immediately on the table after the procedure. I wanted to save patients like she does. It was very cool to witness those miracle moments.

I would choose Neurosurgery field instead of Neurology if I were to go back in time. I was afraid of long hours of operation and didn't think that I would be strong enough for neurosurgery field when I was a medical student.

I have learned that we are interdependent. No one can work alone. Teamwork really makes all the difference. The greatest lesson this profession taught me is taking care of your team well.

My parents and the challenging work I encounter each day push me to get up and keep going at being a Neurologist. I love learning and improving my knowledge and skills. The more patients I see, the more procedures I perform. The more I improve, the more I can help patients.

"Tomorrow is your day!" This quote came from a friend who saw me leaving the hospital after a long call night. It reminds me that when I have a tough day or night, tomorrow can be better. It reminds me to keep HOPE alive and do better when I go back the next day.

There are so many good and bad memories during my career. However, the one I often recall is the conversation I had with a patient's mother. My patient, who had a ruptured brain aneurysm, later had a complicated hospital course and didn't make it. I remember walking into the room before he passed away and told his mother that I was very sorry. His mom told me, "Dr. Pan, don't waste your time here. Go SAVE MORE LIVES! Thank you for everything! GO!" I walked out of the room and felt the tears stream down my face.

YES!! Dr. Pan, go save more lives. They need you!

Kessarin Panichpisal, M.D. (Dr. Pan), Physician

I have been a Medical Doctor for 30 years at Chiang Mai University, in Chiang Mai, Thailand. I've been a Vascular Surgeon for 24 years and a Professor of Surgery for 14 years. I have a great passion for treating patients and training my medical students.

If you have passion and burning desire in your work, even in difficult things, then it is like you play all the time. You would enjoy it and do not want anything in return. I think passion is the most important thing that motivates me up to this day.

My great mentor is Dr. Rabieb Rerkasem, my father. He passed away some 40 years ago. At that time, I was only a 12-year-old boy. He was very passionate about treating patients. He had been the very first qualified general surgeon (from USA) in Chiang Mai and in the northern part of Thailand in 1955. He worked so hard, and he was called by his patients and their families as Dad in Chiang Mai. One time he had a Chinese patient with sepsis foot due to diabetes. My father advised him to have his leg amputated. Before the patient went to the operating room, he told his family that if he died, they must respect Dr. Rabieb Rerkasem like they would respect him as their father. Luckily, his operation was uneventful. However, my dad passed way due to lung cancer a few years later. This Chinese man sat in front of my dad's coffin then cried and cried. He kept saying, "Rabieb, why did you die? I should have died before you did."

I have inherited my dad's passion for treating patients. I have been visiting hemodialysis patients in the 12 provinces in the northern part of Thailand for more than 10 years including the COVID period. The service is a mobile medical unit during my holiday and free of charge. An estimated 40-150 patients came to see me each day. One time I had this service to a city name Phra Yao which is around 200 kilometers from my home. As I was leaving the examination room at the end of working at this service, one of my patients came and asked my colleague which teacup on the table was mine. My colleague was caught by surprise but she indicated that my cup was the white cup. The patient then took a sip of tea from my white cup. He said, "I want my family and my children to be good and sharp like Dr. Kittipan Rerkasem." This experience, although it might not be hygienic and healthy, brought "love" to my heart.

~Kittipan Rerkasem, MD, PhD, Physician

━━━━━➤◆◀━━━━━

I love to help people by using both my medical knowledge and my hand skills. I've been a Surgeon for 13 years and an Oncoplastic Breast Surgeon for seven years. I would not change anything.

I am motivated by knowing that my patients can go home with smiles and can live happily after the surgery.

I have learned that operating the disease is not the same as treating the patient. Trying to understand a patient from all dimensions is more difficult than just giving them treatment. You want to be a real doctor and not just a drug seller.

A memorable experience for me involves my end stage breast cancer patient. She was able to pass away happily (which was her intention) with perfect breast morphology after the breast cancer surgery.

~Kraipope Jarupaiboon, Physician

"An opportunity comes to a prepared mind." This inspirational quote is from one of my mentors.

I have been an Associate Professor and a Medical Practitioner for two decades. My current job positions allow me to conduct research while doing clinical practice at the same time. On one end, the majority of my work has been about health services research. That gives me a great opportunity to explore the whole healthcare system from the perspective of various stakeholders. I also have a chance to encourage and support junior researchers and medical students who would like to have hands-on research experience. On the other end, my clinical work ranges from general medical check-ups during the daytime to emergency care during the nighttime. Both ends harmonize making me a clinician who can see the big picture and a researcher with a realistic perception of medical care. An alternative job for my past self could have been an economist.

There have been many lessons in my life. The greatest one is about surviving my career through various types of people, especially those who do not like me or what I am. One of the best solutions I have learned is to change an enemy into a friend.

I guess the fear of failure gets me going and the sense of hopeful success motivates me.

My memorable experiences include: (1) as a clinician, when I successfully resuscitate my patients; and (2) as a researcher, when I am successfully published in a good journal.

~ Krit Pongpirul, Physician

I find this quote from His Royal Highness Prince Mahidol of Songkla inspirational.
"Being a physician is an honorable job.
A good physician is not rich but not poor.
Being a physician must be kind and has idealism."

I have been a Trauma Surgeon for 23 years. It is both a challenge and a privilege to help people. This job gives me the opportunity to help patients during the worst times of their lives and help them return home to be with their families.

I have never regretted even one second of my life working as a Trauma Surgeon. I am full of joy every time I save my injured patients, or see them awake and smiling at their families and friends.

I believe that when we have to make a decision during critical moments in life, we may have multiple options. We must be logical and make a choice based on our intuition, careful consideration, and our experience. We must make a decision because indecision could cause a delay and it may result in harm to ourselves and others.

Every time I fail, make a mistake, or didn't get what I wish for, I always think that it is my fate or destiny from a higher power. I strongly believe that if we do good things for others, never do harm, and don't take advantage of others, we would find that good things come back to us.

Whatever happened to us during the bad times or during our failures will eventually lead us to a better position.

I'll never forget my birthday a few years ago when I was on call. That night, a 14-year-old girl was severely injured in a T-bone car accident. She was in a very critical condition, having lost massive amounts of blood in her abdomen from an injury to her spleen. She was in shock and required emergent surgery to remove her spleen and stop the bleeding. After surgery, she remained unstable in ICU for several days. Our trauma team did our best to save her life and after almost three weeks, she survived! She was able to continue her junior year in high school. Later, she came back to visit me at the hospital, telling me that she wanted to study Medicine in the future. She realized that doctors save lives and give new lives to injured patients. She said, "The day I had an accident was not only your birthday; it was my birthday for my new life as well. I will use my new life to do good deeds for other people."

~Narain Chotirosniramit, Physician

I'm a Pediatric Neurologist and Assistant Professor of Clinical Neurology at the University of Miami. I finished my training 10 years ago and have been practicing at UM since 2011.

I chose Pediatrics because, in the words of my medical school's Chair of Pediatrics, I liked kids... but hated adults. Pediatrics felt fresh and exciting because I could choose to look at the world through my patients' eyes. I didn't consider Neurology until later, but was always fascinated with the developing brain. Once I figured this all out, Pediatric Neurology seemed like it was tailor-made for me.

I would choose this profession again in a heartbeat. I have the best job in the world! But, in another world, I would like more time (and inspiration) to write and to bake.

It would be easy to say my family motivates me. Of course, that is always true. But, aside from that, it comes down to the knowledge that there is a job and it needs to be done. If I don't do it, who will? I do my part so that everyone else can do theirs.

My most memorable experience in this profession was the time a terrified child refused to talk to the residents or the attending pediatrician. Instead, the child chose to trust me (a pediatric intern at the time) with her secrets. I still don't know why I was the only one she would talk to, but I've never forgotten it.

Medicine is a language. We learn the vocabulary in medical school and grammar in residency. Our job is to translate it into words that our patients and their families can understand. That way,
we can make knowledgeable decisions together.

"Since no one is perfect, it follows that all great deeds have been accomplished out of imperfection. Yet they were accomplished, somehow, all the same." ~Lois McMaster Bujold. In other words, we don't need perfection. Do your best, and get the job done.

~Paige Kalika, Physician

⟫●⟪

I consider being a physician like being a detective with a stethoscope. In every case, there are clues that I can gather and investigate, then make determinations based on those. That matches my personality perfectly. Moreover, being a physician is life-fulfilling when you know that doing your best everyday can make things better for your patients. That kind of return is much more valuable than money.

Motivations which help me to get up and keep going are my family and patients. I want to make my family proud of what I do— especially my daughter. She is very interested in my work and loves to give her 7-year-old point of view. I would like to set an example for her about hard work and responsibilities.

Another motivation is my concern for patients and their families. I know that having a sick loved one is tough on every member of the family. I always think of how I can best support them so they can have a life as normal as possible.

I have a picture in my head where I see my parents as patients who need help desperately from doctors. My mom was a nurse who took care of her patients with love and a warm heart. Those are what inspire me every day.

I've been a Clinical Geneticist for 14 years. The greatest lesson this job has taught me is teamwork. Respect your colleagues and patients, compromise, and believe in yourself.

One memory that stands out to me was my last week in a clinic as a full-time Genetic Attending Physician. It was an emotional week because I knew I would miss seeing and helping my patients. I also knew I would miss working with my wonderful colleagues on how to solve medical mysteries.

~Pranoot Tanpaiboon, Physician

"What doesn't kill you will only make you
stronger."

I've been a doctor since 2006. My father urged me (if not straight out decided for me) to go to medical school. I enjoy what I do. In the same way a master baker kneads and shapes dough to make a perfect pie, doctors make adjustments to patients' medications. When we witness the patients slowly recuperate, it's very satisfying.

If I go back in time to the same place I was when choosing careers, I probably would not have chosen Medicine. I liked Physics in school. Then again, I may not have gone into science at all!

I'm not sure there is a single greatest lesson this profession has taught me. Every day I learn something new. One must constantly be humble about what she doesn't know and be open to learning from others.

At Long Island College hospital, I did a stroke intervention on a patient with basilar stroke. We got the vessel open but ultimately the patient died. Later, the family talked to me and gave me a pack of socks. They hoped the socks would keep my feet warm because they thought I work hard.

The daughter said, "When I met you at first, I wondered, 'Who is this young person who is going to work on my dad?' But then you came out after the procedure all sweaty."

She said she could see the lines on my face where the mask had been and then she understood that I was trying my best to help her father.

~*Sophia Janjua, Physician*

━━━━━➤◆◆◀━━━━━

The most memorable experience I've had was receiving a card from my patient. It said, "You are a true doctor." I've kept it to this day.

I've been a Physician for more than 30 years. I always wanted to be a physician and I think that I made that decision very early in my life. The reason behind it was my deep sense of compassion and desire to help others. The other reason was that I was always fascinated with the great mystery of life and the human body. I wanted to understand it better.

Even after practicing Medicine for so many years and knowing how hard it can sometimes be, I would still choose the same profession. But if for some reason I had to make a different choice, it would be Archeology.

The greatest lesson I learned is that there is so much more that we do not know and how vulnerable we are.

My motivation to keep going is that I know that there is a patient who is suffering and needs my help.

A colleague once told me this quote that resonated with me: "People do not care how much you know until they know how much you care."

~Vesna Starcevic, Physician

—————>⋙●⋘<—————

Everyone loves to be alive and healthy. Whatever I am able to do to achieve that goal, I do it. I've been a Cardiologist for 14 years.

In Cardiology, I think everything is touchable, logical, and uses less imaginative thinking as compared to other medical fields like Neurology, for example.

Once you are on duty, there is no excuse not to perform your job. This is true even when you are having a troubled personal life situation. You have to forget it and leave it behind because it might make you lose your practice.

My personal quote: "Do the best you can in your practice and you are going to be proud of yourself even if you lose your patient." I also have a quote from the Founder of Modern Thai Medical Education: "Think of others before yourself." I use this as a great reminder in my everyday practice.

A memorable moment for me was when I was able to save my patient who had a cardiac arrest. Eventually, he was able to leave the hospital with full physical and emotional function. He was my first case where I initiated therapeutic hypothermia following the recommended CPR guidelines.

~Wannakorn Phatarajaree, Physician

CHAPTER 30

Public Safety Officer

I was a police officer for about 16 years then I retired. I wanted to make a difference and have a job that could help people in many ways. I applied for the Public Safety Officer position and it has been the best move I have ever done. It's an amazing place to work and grow in a career. I've been a Public Safety Officer here for a year now.

If I could go back in time, I will still choose this job, but I would've chosen it sooner. It is a no-brainer. It's an amazing career where you get to meet new people, get to help patients, get to talk to visitors, and help your fellow employees. It's a rewarding career.

The biggest lesson that I've learned is that we're dealt curveballs in our careers and in life. We just have to figure out a way to hit the ball and strive for that goal. Don't let anybody tell you that you can't achieve it. If you put your mind to it, you will achieve and conquer, and become a great leader. Nothing is ever handed to you. You have to earn everything.

My family and my coworkers are amazing and they keep me going. I don't wanna let them down. If I'm not here, my boss Chris and Alex have been really good for the department. Most of all, it's the patients who motivate me. I want to see them smile when they leave by the direction that they have with Public Safety and the staff.

Don't ever let anybody tell you that you can't achieve what you want in life.

There was an elderly lady with Dementia and she was lost in the hospital. She left the property. The whole Public Safety Staff and Dispatcher did everything in their power to find her. The patient was later located a couple of blocks away. The feeling of being able to do everything in your power as a team to find her and bring her home safely was the biggest achievement I think we've had so far.

~ Jimmy Sanchez, Public Safety Officer

CHAPTER 31

Radiology Technologists

I'm a CT Technologist and I've been here for a year.

I went through x-ray school here at Aurora St. Luke's Medical Center and rotated through the CT department here. Once I rotated through the CT department, I was really drawn to that side of imaging versus x-ray. I really enjoyed the clinical aspect of CT. I liked how it combined aspects of both patient care on a whole different level than x-ray and how technicians manipulate the machines to get the best images. The different exams and even procedures really interested me as a student. I decided to spend even more time here as a student and then when I graduated, I applied for an open position here.

I always wanted to make a difference in the lives of others. Being able to work for and care for patients and be that person to make a difference in their time here at the hospital has always been rewarding to me.

I've learned that it's okay to make mistakes. That is the one thing that really stuck with me through x-ray school and my training here in CT. Everyone makes mistakes. The biggest thing is to admit when you make one and learn from it. It will only make you a better tech.

I find this quote inspirational: "There are no secrets to success. It is the result of preparation, hard work and learning from failure." ~Colin Powell

After doing a scan on a patient, he told me that he was very dizzy and wasn't feeling the best. We got on the topic of getting something to eat. I offered him a sandwich from our nursing observation area. He was so thankful and happy about it. I remember he went right out into the waiting room and started to eat. It really warmed my heart because I took that short time to just chat with the patient to learn he hadn't eaten all day. It really is the little things.

~Amanda R Hetzel, Radiology Technologist

I am a Mammography Technologist. I have been in this role for four years.

I love helping people and being a Mammographer gives me the opportunity to play a direct role in my patient's health and wellness. I just really enjoy knowing that my job helps save lives and that what I'm doing every day really makes an impact. We can all make a difference in someone's life— big or small.

"Be kind!" Not sure where or who this quote is from but I just love the simplicity of it and how impactful being kind truly is.

~Anonymous 1, Radiology Technologist

⎯⎯⎯⎯⎯⎯⎯⎯

I've been an Interventional Radiologic Technologist for two years and 11 months. I wanted to be involved in direct patient care that showed immediate results. If I could go back in time, I would have become a Vet.

The quote that inspires me is: "Do unto others as you would have them do unto you." I want to be helpful and I hope that the care I provide will one day be returned to me or a loved one.

Illness affects anyone and everyone at some point, whether directly or indirectly. We rely on healthcare workers to provide the best care for a positive outcome.

Every positive outcome is memorable, whether it's an emergent bleed, Transjugular intrahepatic portosystemic shunt (TIPS) or stroke. When our actions create a positive outcome for a patient, it's not only memorable, but fulfilling.

~Anonymous 2, Radiologic Technologist

———⟫◈⟪———

I am a CT technologist and I have been doing this for about two years now. I love Medicine and I love helping people. With this job, I feel like I am able to help people by giving the doctors' knowledge about what could be causing their ailments. I absolutely love what I do! I don't think I can see myself doing anything different in my career.

I have learned patience. Even though most of the day we are asked to do more and get more people scanned, I have learned that with a little bit of patience, we can get more accomplished than if we rushed.

What keeps me going is the unknown about the person who will cross through my CT doors. Everyone has their own personal anatomy, their own persona, and it's always fun to meet new people.

My favorite quote that I saw one time read, "Never let success get to your head. Never let failure get to your heart."

The most memorable experience in my career has to be the day I helped a Russian-speaking patient be comfortable with a CT scan. She was in a tremendous amount of anxiety from previous results and just wanted to get out of the scanner. I reassured her that we would be taking excellent care of her. I was able to guide her through the scanning process to get her the best results possible.

~Anonymous 3, Radiology Technologist

I wanted to work in healthcare, but did not want to be a nurse. I job shadowed here at St. Luke's and eventually got into our X-ray program. During clinicals, I rotated through CT several times and loved it. Immediately following graduation, I took a position in the CT department. I've been a CT Technologist for six years.

I've learned that coming in each day with a positive attitude can greatly help shape the types of days you will have. Care and compassion should be leading qualities we use to care for our patients.

"Create a life you can't wait to wake up to." (Found on Pinterest.) It feels good to get up and be able to go to a job that I love, knowing that I could potentially make a difference for even just one patient. It makes it worth it.

A couple of years ago, I had a patient who was extremely claustrophobic and terrified to have a CT scan. She was almost in tears. We took an extensive amount of time to explain everything and prepare her for what was coming next. We got her through the exam. I don't remember what type of exam she was having done, but I do remember how grateful and appreciative she was when it was over. She thanked us endlessly for helping her get through it. Her response to us caring for her is something I won't forget.

~Ashley Schneider, Radiology Technologists

I've been a Nuclear Medicine Technologist for 30 years. I knew I wanted to do something in healthcare. I was at UW Lacrosse which had the program. I switched from physical therapy.

Over the years, I have come to meet and interact with more upper-level management and administration as well as the processes involved with upper-level decision making. I have come to the conclusion that, for the most part, the success of healthcare institutions and most of the positive outcomes happen from the day-to-day efforts of individuals at lower levels. I used to assume the people at these upper levels must be so smart and dedicated and hardworking and unselfish. Were the policies and decisions a careful balance of concern and empathy for patients and staff? Do they offer the best options financially for the institution? Unfortunately, I think, not so much. Success and positive patient outcomes come mostly in spite of these people and their decisions and because of the daily efforts of first level people directly involved in patient care.

Daily interactions with patients and staff are what keep me motivated. A sum of hundreds or thousands of positive interactions of meeting interesting people, staff and patients, and helping and sharing in their life— these make up my most memorable experiences in this career.

~Bernard Koch, Radiology Technologist

The first time I saw a cerebral angiogram during my clinical training, I was fascinated. Seeing firsthand the effects of removing a clot from someone's brain and seeing the patient talk minutes after the clot removal made me want to do this for the rest of my career. I've been a Neuro Interventional Radiology Technologist for 23 years.

The greatest lesson I've learned in my professional life is to not always be the first person to talk and to step back and observe your surroundings.

My inspirational quote is, "Learning something today will prepare you for tomorrow." My motivation to keep going is knowing that every day, I have the opportunity to learn something new and to share that knowledge.

About 15 years ago, I was involved in a stroke case. The patient came into the room aphasic and not communicative. I recall the procedure was less than an hour but when we were finished, the patient began talking and communicating with all of us within minutes of the procedure ending. That was my first real memorable experience with strokes and the positive effects that we have on patients. To see a person start talking after the removal of a clot from their brain was very memorable.

~Dave Smith, Radiology Technologist

I am an Interventional Radiologic Technologist. I have been doing this for almost five years (It'll be five years in February). I chose this job because I love helping people and I knew I wanted a job in healthcare. I went into x-ray school after I earned my bachelor's degree from UW Madison and was lucky to get this job as my first one out of x-ray school. If I could go back in time, I would definitely still choose this job.

The greatest lesson I have learned is that everyone might have a different way of doing some tasks, or have different problem-solving skills, but I think we all try to work towards the same goal of providing the best patient care possible.

I like the quote by Anne Frank that states, "Whoever is happy will make others happy too." I really enjoy the type of work we do and I love helping people feel better. I also get along with everyone I work with and love working with them so that motivates me and makes it easy to keep going.

I can't think of a specific memorable experience in my career but I do remember the good feelings I get when I can help hold someone's hand or reassure patients when they are scared during their procedure or time in the hospital.

~*Emily Hinds, Radiologic Technologist*

I have been Radiologic Technologist for over 13 years. I joined the Interventional Radiology team six years ago. I chose my career in healthcare because caring for people and being around people is something I greatly enjoy. Having a career that allows me to help others and care for them is extremely uplifting. If I could go back in time, I would've chosen to start this career earlier in my life.

My motivating factors are the thought that my actions and that my interaction with others can make a difference. Every time I can make somebody else smile and feel better, I get very motivated to keep pushing forward. I try to make a difference with at least one person every day.

"One smile or one listening ear sometimes can chase away someone's fear." I find these words very inspiring.

Always be kind. People may be fighting battles that we know nothing about. Smiles can be contagious and the way you handle the situation and help another person can literally change their life.

My most memorable moment was when I was in x-ray school. There was a technician teaching me and she was getting upset with a patient who was being rather mean. The technician walked away and I started talking to the patient. She was not happy that we had asked her to remove her bra for a chest x-ray. I simply asked her why she had a problem with this and explained we needed this x-ray for her doctor. She then started to explain to me that she had breast cancer that she found out had just come back. She was being mean because she was hurting. After talking to her and listening to her she then complied with removing her bra for the exam. By the end of the exam, she was thanking me and smiling. That gave me the most incredible feeling and I will never forget it.

~Jennifer Bond, Radiologic Technologist

———⟫◆⟪———

I am a Nuclear Medicine Technologist. I have been a tech for over 40 years. I like to say the job chose me. I went to school to become a Medical Technologist, but I was unable to find an internship. I had never heard of this field but a nun came up to me and showed me a brochure describing it. I applied and got in. I have never looked back. You really have to enjoy your job to be able to do it well. It really shows if you don't care.

I am glad I am in the field now. I can tell lots of stories from the olden days and how much things have changed over time.

This is my favorite quote: "You gotta do what you gotta do!"

Having a purpose in life is my biggest motivator. I was off for a few weeks on furlough during the pandemic and I really felt lost, like my life had no meaning. I had plenty of things to do at home but being at work was a lifesaver.

I would say my most memorable experience was when I was involved in research at the old Mount Sinai Hospital. We worked on developing the first artificial heart. I was just involved in the testing of it, a very minor role. But knowing that I played a very minute part was neat.

~Kay Maracini, Radiology Technologist

I'm an Interventional Radiology Technologist. I have been doing this for a little over a year.

I chose this job because it fits me well as a person. I'm a people person. I love to help out as much as possible and hands-on is a must for me. I like to have patient interaction and be an active party when treating a patient. This job fits me well because it feels good to know I am part of a team that prevented something bad from happening.

If I could go back in time, I'd most likely still choose this job. I love the workflow and how we're always moving and doing something and not waiting for something to happen.

Every situation is different and all you can do is be kind to anyone and everyone, coworkers and patients altogether. No one knows their story and what they've gone through. The best I can do as a healthcare worker is to be the little light that shines and hopefully brightens their day.

I feel like every experience here is very memorable. Day in and day out, we never know if we'll be getting a very sick patient or not until it becomes an emergent case. Most of our patients are fairly well and walking and/or talking patients. It's a very satisfying feeling when you get that emergent bleed and know that you've done your part to help and prevent a bad outcome.

Coming to work and knowing I've made a difference in my patients' lives and seeing coworkers— that's what motivates me to get up and keep going.

I don't have an original quote but something that motivates me constantly is "Keep moving forward. There will always be a light waiting at the end of the tunnel." I'm not sure where I heard it from, but I've constantly reminded myself of it every time I feel like I've hit a wall.

~Lee Vang, Radiology Technologist

I am an Interventional Radiology (IR) Technologist and have been doing this for six years. When I went through IR for x-ray school, I knew it is what I wanted to pursue. I loved the teamwork, working closely with the doctors, seeing the good patient outcomes, and really feeling accomplished after every case. The high pace environment for emergencies is energizing and addictive. I would most definitely choose this job again. The only other profession I would love to try would be an EMT.

Besides the patients we take care of day in and day out, my husband and daughter motivate me. In the recent weeks, everyone has become grateful for all healthcare workers and for what we do. I always tell my family and friends that we do it for the patients because it's 100% true. If you aren't in it to help people, you are in the wrong career.

The only quote that has really stuck with me is "If at first you don't succeed, try, try again." This was said by an American educator, Thomas H. Palmer. This profession also taught me not to underestimate yourself. If you put your mind to something and want it, don't let anyone tell you different.

There have been quite a few very memorable moments in my four-year career. Most have been while I was working with the Neurointerventional team. We've been doing stroke intervention on a middle-aged woman. A few days later, she walked into our department with her family behind her and they thanked us. Tears were falling. My coworkers and I didn't have a dry eye either. I still get goosebumps telling this story because it shows firsthand how thankful the patients are for what we do. It also shows how we can truly save lives. This woman could have lost the ability to walk, talk, eat, or worse, may not have survived at all. But because of the team's great work, she can walk and hug her family again. This memory is why we love what we do.

~Lindsey Haas, Radiology Technologist

I always wanted to do something to help people out. I changed careers in my late 20s/early 30s. I was a mortgage and loan banker for about 10 years but hated what I did. I decided to volunteer at a hospital and I just fell in love with procedural stuff. I wanted to make more of a positive difference in people's lives. I went back to school and got my license and certification in X-ray and MRI. Then I was introduced to Interventional Radiology (IR) and Cath Lab. I absolutely fell in love with that. Now, doing Neuro, I love how much I've learned in the past 3-4 years. I'm a Neurovascular & Endovascular Interventional Technologist RT(IR) and I've been in this role for three years.

I would choose my profession over and over and over again. I honestly wish that I was introduced to this earlier or knew that it existed sooner because it's definitely what I've always wanted to do. No one in high school or in grade school ever talks about this kind of stuff as a career choice.

My wife and two daughters keep me going. Everything I do, I do for them. I just want to make my two daughters proud.

"Don't limit your challenges. Challenge your limits." I heard this quote somewhere and it stuck. I've always tried to be fearless and confident to try anything.

Be constantly willing to challenge yourself to do better. Be constantly willing to learn and accept constructive criticism so that you can get better not only as a person but as a worker/technologist. Also, listen more than speak. You can pick up so much just by listening to people around you.

Not everyone you help will make it through or get better from their condition. Be accepting of that and know there will be times when it will be tough. There are those who won't get better. But even if only one person does, it's worth it!

It's remarkable to see patients recover and do better after doing a case. It's most memorable when you see them after the fact.

~Manny Zaica, Radiology Technologist

———»●«———

I'm a Neurovascular Clinical Specialist. I have worked in healthcare for 14 years, and as a Radiologic Technologist for 10 years.

I come from a long line of nurses and originally was going to go that route. After doing phlebotomy and working as a tech assistant in Interventional Radiology (IR), I decided that I might enjoy a job that had a little less of the in-depth direct patient care. I was in favor of a more technology-driven career. My mother, who was a nurse in IR at the time, thought it would be a great career choice for me. Having been on the nursing track for 25 years, she thought I would be more interested in IR more than in Nursing.

As far as healthcare goes, I am very happy with my decision. I think a lot of people wish they maybe had gone further with their education sooner. I have always been interested in the role of a Physician's Assistant, but I also enjoy the level of controlled stress that my job allows. I do not leave work questioning myself or feeling stressed. Outside of healthcare, I would love to work in forestry or with animals in any capacity. But I wouldn't change my job security or the personal fulfillment either.

As a traveler, I really learned to stay very, very humble. There are people who will know more than you or have a different or better way of doing something. So much can be learned from others to make you a better professional and caregiver.

I also learned that so many people suffer from "impostor syndrome", myself included. We know we went through school, did the work, and got the job. But often, we feel like everyone else is a little more knowledgeable or more able than we are. We think at some point someone is going to realize that you shouldn't be doing the job. So many people have that fear of not being good enough or smart enough. They are just waiting for someone to figure it out. We ALL feel this way at some point but it does go away with years of experience and confidence-building situations.

What keeps me going is the impact that our care has on our patients and their families. We have to be there for them on what is sometimes the worst days of their lives. I also feel a commitment to my coworkers and our providers to support them in serving our community. Also, I am not going to sugarcoat it, but it's the paycheck. I have to be there to support myself and my family. Fortunately, there is a level of comfort and security that comes from working in healthcare.

I worked with Dr. Jerry Michel, a wonderful physician from Everett, Washington. He would often tell me, "There is no traffic on the extra mile!" He would say it whenever I would go above and beyond. It felt good to be acknowledged. It reminded me to always make that extra effort. While we hope everyone will do those extra things, sometimes they don't. You may be that one person making a difference.

I don't have a most memorable experience or patient, though many have left imprints on me. At the end of the day, my coworkers from across the country and a few of the physicians who have mentored me have meant the most to me. They helped me become the best version of myself as a technologist and that is my most cherished experience.

~Megan Smith, Radiologic Technologist

I have been a CT + MRI Technologist for 15 years. I always had an interest in the medical field and radiology seemed like the right fit. I have learned so much and grown so much from this profession.

These two quotes have always inspired me:

"When you see someone without a smile,
give them one of yours!"

"It's not about how you fall. It's about how
you get back up."

Every day you have the ability to make a positive difference in someone's life. I would say that you need to be 100% responsible for the energy and attitude you bring into the work space-- for your coworkers AND for your patients. Your attitude and energy can completely make or break your day or your patient's experience with you. BE RESPONSIBLE! BE POSITIVE.

There were a few repeat patients I've had who have been the most beautiful spirits! I was able to connect with them and get to know them a little more each time they came. They were able to maintain so much positivity even though they were ill and fighting against various illnesses and terminal diseases. I will never forget them!

~Michelle Efta, Radiology Technologist

I've been a CT Technologist for two years. Throughout my high school, I had a passion for enriching my knowledge in health, anatomy and physiology, and medical technology. I decided to apply my interest in medicine and technology in radiography school. Once I finished X-ray school, I decided to pursue CT (CAT SCAN).

Every day I learn something new at my job. I learn a lot from experience itself and from all the types of scans we do. We also have so many resources. We get to speak to radiologists, radiology residents, and some of the doctors who put in the orders for a CT on a patient. One of the reasons I enjoy my job is that I am able to collaborate with doctors in finding what's best for the patient. We have to adjust some scan protocols based on the indications and what the doctor is trying to find. To do so, doctors usually need to discuss this with the radiologists. That collaboration is awesome.

These are the greatest lessons I've learned in this profession: Don't ever get too high and don't ever get too low. There will be good days and bad days. Roll with the punches and embrace change.

I try to maintain perspective. I'm going to work hard at what I signed up for. Someone else might not be as fortunate to even have the opportunity to do what we do in the medical field. I also know my limits and understand when to stop and breathe.

"Don't ever lose your smile." When I worked at a retirement home, a resident said that to me on one of the last days I worked there. I sometimes use that quote and that memory through challenging moments at work.

The memories that I hold tight are the moments that bring my co-workers and me closer together, through good times and bad times. When patients tell us their stories and thank us for our services, that always feels rewarding as well.

~*Ryan Below, Radiology Technologist*

Chapter 32

Registered Cardiovascular Invasive Specialist

This is my personal quote:

> "The path to success is paved with struggles.
> You may have taken the wrong path if you
> desire to succeed but are not struggling."

I have been a Registered Cardiovascular Invasive Specialist for six years. My biggest motivators in this job are my family and my patients. I chose this profession to contribute to humanity and save lives, as helping others brings me joy.

I once told a heart attack patient, "Sorry, I have to cut your shirt." I took a pair of scissors, cut his T-shirt, quickly applied the defibrillator pads, and moved on with the rescue procedure.

After we opened the blocked artery and saved his life, he told me, "This was my favorite shirt."

"Sorry, your shirt was sacrificed so you can live," I replied.

Three hours later, we received a call from the patient's nurse in the ICU, who told us the patient was asking if the entire team could come to his room to sign his shirt. He was going to hang the autographed shirt on the wall at home. So, we did.

~Mohamed B. Hommeida,
Registered Cardiovascular Invasive Specialist

CHAPTER 33

Registered Dental Hygienist

"Healthy teeth make healthy smiles."

I love teeth and people. I feel dental health is very important for our overall health. I'm a Registered Dental Hygienist. I graduated from Marquette University in 1993.

The greatest lesson I've learned in my professional life is dealing with all types of people and all that comes with that.

Knowing that every day I am making a difference with each patient motivates me to get up and keep going.

Being President of the Marquette University Dental Hygiene Alumni Association is my most memorable experience in my career.

~Heidi Huebschen, Registered Dental Hygienist

CHAPTER 34

Rehabilitation Aide

"Clouds come floating into my life, no longer to carry the rain or usher storm, but to add color to my sunset sky."

I am a Rehabilitation Aide and I have worked at St. Luke's in this job for 34 years. When I applied, it was for a completely different job. I can't remember what it was, but I received a call that there was an opening as a Rehabilitation Aide and I took it.

If I could go back, I would definitely go to school and get some kind of medical degree. I would still choose this job because I love what I do!

These days it's not easy to come to work with everything going on, but I know that I truly make a difference for all my patients.

I have learned that everyone has value and that everyone contributes to the patient experience. For me, memorable experiences include those instances when I am able to provide something to patients who could not do things for themselves.

~Anonymous 1, Rehabilitation Aide

I'm a Rehabilitation Aide and have worked in this position at Aurora for about 10 years. I was a Massage Therapist for 30 years. To me, my job is meaningful when I am able to assist therapists in helping patients.

This profession has taught me so much about patience.

Christian living and faith are what motivate me to keep going. I turn to Psalms and Proverbs for daily inspiration..

If I were to go back in time, I might be a pottery artist.

~Anonymous 2, Rehabilitation Aide

Chapter 35

Researcher

I found research very fascinating. I have been working in Academic Research for the past 11 years. In order to gain in-depth knowledge and to advance my career, I chose to attend graduate school. I started graduate school in 2019.

I will definitely choose pursuing research again. However, If I am given an option to time travel, I would have chosen to be a physician. I feel it is the most mentally rewarding job anyone can wish for.

My passion for what I do drives me forward. Despite the hurdles I've come across in my life, my positive attitude and strong faith in myself motivate me every day. Whenever I lose self-confidence, my inner self pushes me with this thought: "Nothing is impossible in this world if you have the true passion, love, and sincerity to do it."

I'm also inspired by the words: "No matter what, this day shall also pass and tomorrow is a new beginning."

One has to be true to oneself and to others. Love your job and spread your positivity around. These are the greatest lessons I have learned in this job.

The most memorable experience in my career was back in 2009, when my first research finding was published.

~Reji Babygrija, Researcher

CHAPTER 36

Speech Language Pathologist

I have been working as a Speech Language Pathologist (SLP) for seven years. My sister, a Physical Therapist, recommended I look into Speech Therapy. I have had an interest in the functional abilities of the brain after watching a family member progress through the stages of Alzheimer's.

I certainly would choose this profession all over again. I get great satisfaction seeing patients meet their goals, especially when it promotes connections to family members. I believe that cognitive rehabilitation and dysphagia therapy directly impact people's enjoyment of life. I am happy to have the opportunity to be part of that process.

I have learned that you never know what's important to other people. It is important to understand other people's goals. It directs so much of their behavior and motivation.

Knowing that when I show up to work, I can make a person's day better— that's what keeps me going.

I'll always remember helping a patient identify their Places of Articulation (POA) through alphabet scanning. The patient had the capacity to make decisions but could only volitionally control a vertical eye gaze.

I am inspired by the saying, "When there is an elephant in the room, don't look for monkeys!"

~Bridget Patek, Speech Language Pathologist

CHAPTER 37

Surgery Schedulers

I am a Surgery Scheduler in the Main Operating Room. I have been in this position for almost a year. I was previously a Clinical Office Assistant. I felt I needed more of a challenge. Don't get me wrong. I love my job, but I wouldn't choose to be in this position if I were to travel back in time. I would LOVE to be a Nurse. Although not directly, I do help patients by scheduling their surgeries through the doctor's office. I would enjoy being more on the other side, assisting them for their surgeries.

I have learned that there's no limit to what you can learn, especially when working in the medical field.

My eagerness to learn more pushes me to keep going. Every day is a new day to learn something new. Life is too precious and sometimes we don't appreciate it as much as we should.

My favorite quote: "Work hard in silence. Let your success be your noise."

~Stephanie Juarez, Surgery Scheduler

I am a Surgery Scheduler and I have been doing this since 2005.

I didn't really choose this position…it kind of just fell into my lap! I was originally hired by the Medical College of WI for something completely different. The Surgery Scheduler ended up quitting, so they changed my position.

Since I didn't choose this job in the first place, it's hard to say what I would rather be if I were to go back in time. But I do love what I do!

This profession has taught me to own up to my mistakes and learn from them. I think it's hard for anyone to admit a mistake, but we are all human, so it's going to happen.

Here's a statement that has helped me in this career: "Surround yourself with people who are only going to lift you higher."

I think our department is truly memorable…in everything that we do. I have been lucky to work with amazing people.

What motivates me to get up and keep going? My children for sure. I am a single mother of three, I work two jobs, and I am back in school full time to become a surgical technician. I want to show them that hard work and determination pays off.

~Stephanie Sanders, Surgery Scheduler

Acknowledgements

First, I would like to thank Peggy Johnson, my life coach, who helped me with planning this book project. Special thanks to all the contributors who took the time to share their wonderful experiences, insights, and inspirations. This book would not have been possible without their kindness. Extra special thanks to my editor Donna Goff who helped me tremendously in polishing and formatting the content. Special thanks to Jennifer Maas who gave me advice about the horse and book cover. Profound appreciation goes to Dr. Techatat Techasane, Dr. Nazli Janjua, Dr. Amin Kassam, Dr. Thomas Wolfe and my mentors for believing in me. I am grateful for their encouragement and support. Thank you to my patients and family members, all of whom I have been privileged to serve. Thank you also to all team members that I work with at Aurora St. Luke's Hospital. I am so honored to work alongside you. Finally, to my mom and dad— thank you for your endless love, support, and encouragement. You both are my life-long cheerleaders! Love you mom and Love you dad!

About The Author

Kessarin Panichpisal, MD is a board-certified internist, vascular neurologist, and interventional neurologist. She studied medicine at Chiang Mai University in Thailand and completed her Internal Medicine residency at Texas Tech University. She was a chief neurology resident and vascular neurology fellow at SUNY Downstate Medical Center and interventional neurology fellow at Asia Pacific Comprehensive Stroke Institute in Pomona, CA. Her first book, "BEFAST FOR STROKE" coloring book was specifically designed for stroke prevention. Believing in the power of teamwork, she introduced the concept of "Team Goose" at the hospital where she and her colleagues care for acute stroke patients. Emulating the exceptional behavior of geese in flight, they commit to support one another in achieving their shared purpose. Hence, their Team Goose slogan is "We fight stroke together!" She currently lives in Milwaukee, Wisconsin.

Made in the USA
Monee, IL
13 October 2022

15785497R00206